A RADICAL PROPOSAL
For Full Use of Free Speech

A Radical Proposal

For Full Use of Free Speech

by

STEPHEN T. CLAFLIN, Jr.

PHILOSOPHICAL LIBRARY

NEW YORK

Published 1979 by PHILOSOPHICAL LIBRARY, INC.,
15 East 40 Street, New York, N. Y. 10016

Copyright 1979 by Stephen T. Claflin Jr.

Library of Congress Catalog Card No. 79-84849
SBN 8022-2246-3

Manufactured in the United States of America

Contents

Introduction

In the United States, we pride ourselves on having the right of free speech. However, on close examination, we may find that those who should make the maximum use of their right actually use only half of their right of free speech.

In social or family activity, most people express opinions, explain opinions and ask others to explain. In most private conversations people can freely express opinions that reading standards in schools should be raised, that more efforts should be made to conserve energy, that trade with Russia will bring, or improve, "détente," that we should or shouldn't "trust the Russians" in arms control treaties. Others may ask that such statements be explained in terms of reported facts. We don't hesitate to make statements, explain them and ask others to do the same. In private conversation we make full use of free speech.

Those engaged in business, in making policy decisions for corporations, express ideas and opinions as part of their jobs in almost any level of responsibility. In meetings and conferences, ideas for solving problems or for developing products or services are expressed, questioned, explained and discussed until they are accepted or rejected. The normal responsibilities of those running a business, such as an advertising firm or a department store, or an institution, such as a university, include the full use of free speech.

In family, social and business affairs, we generally don't limit ourselves to expressing our ideas. We also discuss them. Most people in responsible positions in a business don't express ideas unless they are prepared to explain them and answer questions about them. In a corporation, for example, the right to express ideas on policy carries with it the responsibility to explain the ideas. Asking questions about ideas is an equally important responsibility. It would be a strange family or business situation indeed where people only expressed ideas, never asking or answering questions about them.

Wherever there is restraint on full discussion, whether in family, social or business matters, it is generally considered an unhealthy sign. There are generally warnings against adverse consequences. Arbitrary limits on free speech are often thought of as hazards.

However, we seem to accept limitations on dialogue about domestic and foreign policy matters. These limitations on public questions and answers don't seem to worry the influential leaders and thinkers. There is little discussion of national policy, in public media, which corresponds to the give-and-take in private conversation and in making business decisions. There is little public dialogue for the purpose of learning whether statements about national aims and policy can be reconciled with reported facts. There is little expressed concern over the limited use of free speech in this area.

What do we get instead of questions and answers about national policy? Usually two things. One is the television "documentary" or "report" which promises to answer a question on a controversial subject. It can be on anything from the price of natural gas to civil defense against nuclear war. This first substitute for dialogue may also take the form of a newspaper or magazine summary of opposing views in a disputed issue. But if the viewer or reader expects questions and answers on which to base a judgment, the result is bound to be disappointing.

What the general public probably gets is not dialogue but monologues or summaries. In television presentations, the opposing views are often strung together with some attempt at continuity, to create the effect of a dialogue. But what's wrong with dialogue? It is almost as if the broadcasters are making the presentation appear to be what they know it should be. Why make it appear as if there is dialogue? Why not have all those experts who give opinions actually talk to each other so the viewers can see what will happen when there really is genuine dialogue with real questions and answers?

The other thing we get instead of real questions and answers is discussion under adverse conditions. It is quite true that influential people do talk to each other but the conditions are rarely ideal or even favorable for the purpose of seeing whether opinions can be reconciled with reported facts. The average election debate or Senate hearing or "Meet the Press" or "The Advocates" format hardly provides an atmosphere that is needed to attempt to reconcile opinions with facts or with other opinions. These formats aren't intended for that purpose. U.S. senators and representatives, for example, frequently talk to newsmen and sometimes talk to newsmen in each other's presence. But they rarely have public dialogue directly with each other, without intermediaries.

The appropriate setting for questions and answers about opinions would require a meeting of people willing to ask and answer questions to see whether ideas can be understood in terms of reported facts and perhaps a moderator to control temptations to lapse into argument or debate (more on these requirements in Chapters 1 and 6). Two U.S. senators, for example, might try to determine which of their opposing views on "détente" can best be explained in terms of those reported facts which are more or less consistent from one news source to another.

This book makes the assumption that if opinions about domestic and foreign policy are worth expressing in newspapers or on television, they should be sufficiently interesting to be worth discussing for a similar audience. Merely expressing opinions may leave a large gap, something missing in our political process.

If influential politicians, scholars and other experts are willing to express opinions, and they generally are, it would seem reasonable that they should be willing to talk to each other, to ask and answer questions about opinions. However, judging from the lack of questions and answers about certain controversial opinions expressed in public, it could be considered a form of mischief or madness to ask people to explain all those ideas they are so fond of repeating.

Hence, the title of this book. It offers a radical proposal that congressmen, scholars and other experts talk to each other, ask and answer questions, publicly, as a means of involving the public in the process of government. This book proposes discussion of often-expressed opinions for public information, to acknowledge the electorate's ultimate responsibility for many basic elements of U.S. domestic and foreign policy. This book proposes discussion to acknowledge our role and responsibility in government, our need to understand opinions, assumptions, slogans, anything which may influence policy decisions.

This is a proposal for full use of free speech. It is based on a layman's estimate of what we are losing through failure to use our rights to the fullest and on an assessment of what we might regain through full use of rights. This is a proposal for full use of freedom of speech, of our communications media and resources, full use of what our social and political system offers us.

Some will say political experts are properly educating us on issues so we can use our political rights and leverage in the intelligent fashion our system demands. This view will be challenged on these pages. Some will say that although there are newspaper columns and magazine articles on sensitive issues of national policy, these issues shouldn't be discussed in public by experts. Others may say there is nothing to discuss, all issues are clearly resolved in the books, articles, columns, speeches and lectures of the influential people. These views will be challenged here. Some will say that if experts are neglecting responsibilities, other experts will challenge them to accept obligations. Examples will be used here to show that when experts dodge responsibility to explain what they say, their colleagues tend to look the other way.

Can opinion A be explained in terms of reports B and C? Can opinions for or against the need to conserve fuel be explained in terms of reported energy shortages? Can opinions for or against the need to change education standards be understood in terms of high school students' reading scores? Can opinions for or against "détente" with Russia be explained in view of reports of the Soviet conventional arms buildup, or other reports? Can opinions about whether we should "trust the Russians" in arms treaties be explained in view of reports about the Kremlin's treatment of Russian and Soviet peoples, and other reports? Where there are unexplained and unresolved opposing views based on the same reported facts, doesn't this tell us something about the need for discussion, for questions and answers among proponents of the differing views?

Some people may say it doesn't matter that statements are made without being explained in terms of reported facts. Some people may say there is no need for discussion among experts, that all we need in order to understand issues are their opposing views based on the same reported facts. Some will say these opinions are enough to enable us to make decisions we need to make as voters and opinion-poll respondents. However, others may believe we can't afford to rely on opinions which haven't been explained in relation to news reports, that influential people should ask each other to explain ideas that leave questions unanswered, that call for explanation.

In order to function, whether in family, social or business responsibilities, we are obliged to make, explain and question statements. Perhaps the same requirements should apply to those influential people who have political responsibilities. Some may say that responsibilities of "experts" and public officials extend only to making statements, not to questioning or explaining them. But why not take the next step? It seems entirely natural and reasonable for responsible people to discuss differences in the opinions they are so eager to offer the public as explanations of the way things are, as explanations of the meaning of reported facts.

Perhaps those who have assumed public responsibility, who have accepted positions of political or intellectual leadership, the politicians, professors, and other experts, also have the responsibility to discuss differences for the benefit of the public they profess to guide and serve. Acceptance of public responsibility may involve public questions and answers about ideas as well as merely expressing opinions and ideas.

In most businesses and institutions, it seems to be management practice to present discussion on policy matters to those who must decide policy, whether individuals, panels or committees. We use free speech to full advantage in making policy in our manufacturing firms and universities.

If corporation policy-makers want to hear, or take part in, discussion before making decisions, perhaps the U.S. voting and opinion-polled public deserves similar consideration on serious matters of national policy. While we may not make policy, we may be required to vote a candidate, and a policy associated with that candidate, up or down in an election. An increasing number of questions may become subject to initiative or referendum. We must ultimately be satisfied with policy, whether it is a policy on energy, education or "détente." Shouldn't we be entitled to make these decisions on the basis of full use of free speech, on the basis of questions and answers, not just somebody's opinion and somebody else's opposing opinion?

It would seem imperative to use free speech to present issues to voters which voters may be called on to decide. Discussion of issues may not be conclusive, may not "prove" anything, but dialogue can indicate that reported facts tend to support one opinion or another. If there is open discussion, facts can tend to support or oppose a new plan offered to decision-makers in a corporation. If there is open discussion, facts can tend to support or oppose the idea that there is, or should be, détente between the U.S. and Russia.

The influential scholars, congressmen and other experts are almost all on record as favoring freedom of speech. But most of them seem to favor its use only up to a point which is far short of any abuse of free speech. Most influential people seem to want to express opinions publicly but show much less enthusiasm for discussing opinions publicly with someone who may disagree. Most seem to favor use of free speech only if it is easy and free of risk, only if they don't have to get involved in asking or answering any questions except the "news conference" kind which usually play leapfrog with various topics without dealing with any subject at any length.

Why shouldn't influential people who make public statements explain them? Why not explain their ideas? Most of the rest of us have to do this. Why not talk publicly to people of opposing views? In private conversation, in family matters and in business affairs most people have to talk to others they disagree with almost every day.

We may have conditioned ourselves to think that what is "normal" for some people is unthinkable for others. Full use of free speech is "normal" in business but not in government. If asking for full use of free speech is a radical proposal, it shows how willingly we have accepted limits on free speech, limits on discussion of differences and, as a probable consequence, limits on ability to solve problems of domestic and foreign policy. Limits on discussion can mean limits on solutions to problems.

Perhaps we need to work toward a state of mind in which discussion of public issues in public isn't a startling notion. If we need all our resources of communication in family relationships and in social and business pursuits, we need all our resources of communication in running our government.

We seem determined to place limits where they can do the most harm. Why do we discuss differences in almost any field of activity *except* the public evaluation of ideas, opinions and assumptions which influence the domestic and foreign policy of the United States? Why limit the use of our greatest national resource when dealing with our most important responsibility?

Some people may say there is no existing opportunity for such direct discussion. However, if there is room in media for opinion, there is room for dialogue. If one person can find a platform for a statement, two or more should be able to find a platform for questions and answers about the statement. Dialogue on opinion should be at least as attention-getting, and salable in print or on the air, as the news report of the opinion itself.

How do we explain the silence, the lack of public dialogue? Do we really believe there is nothing to discuss, that nothing needs to be done to help the public toward a better understanding of issues? Are we acting as if all issues have been settled, that there is nothing to talk about?

A suggestion that we make full use of free speech shouldn't be a radical proposal but for some reason it seems to be just that. How did we come to this state of affairs? It could be due to certain attitudes, habits and taboos which seem to have a firm hold on the influential people in the United States.

A RADICAL PROPOSAL
For Full Use of Free Speech

1

The Rules

In order to protect themselves from the hazards of dialogue, from having to answer obvious questions about their own ideas, the influential people have devised for themselves a set of rules. The Rules are unwritten but very effective. No respectable influential person ever mentions The Rules or even hints they might exist. The Rules nevertheless prevent us from applying the same principles (discussion of views and options in reaching policy decisions) to our society and government that we apply to our businesses and institutions.

For example, although we have the right to discuss national policy in public, on television, we rarely use it. Public discussion of our domestic and foreign policy is limited not by coercion, as in "other countries," but by The Rules which have become binding on influential people in the United States. A college professor may not ask a politician, government official or another professor or some other influential person to explain published statements in a television discussion, especially if the statements seem to be in collision with well-known reported facts. Interviewing etiquette forbids obvious questions. Asking for explanations of statements when they are needed and when none are offered would be legal in the United States but strictly against The Rules.

Whether "détente" between the U.S. and Russia still happens to be a "live issue," it was the subject of many books and articles published in the U.S. during the 1960's and 1970's. It is an example of a subject which could have been discussed publicly for many years. It is a possible solution to a foreign policy problem and it has prominent and articulate supporters and opponents. Over a period of years the public has been urged to support or oppose this or that version of "détente" with the Soviet Union. But how often has the public been offered a basis for judgment? How often is "détente" or any of the related issues discussed in public by people of opposing views?

This is an illustration of a voluntarily accepted limitation of free speech but a limitation which is enshrined in custom. We would be ready to fight anyone who imposed such a limitation on us in the form of a decree. But this doesn't prevent us from accepting The Rules virtually without question.

It is a rare occasion in the U.S. when two influential people meet in a lecture hall, a campus auditorium or in a television studio and one asks the other to reconcile opinions, ideas and slogans with news reports. Such an encounter is even rarer when the two people represent opposing political views. Public discussion among people of differing opinions on national policy seems to be against The Rules.

In a typical televised meeting with reporters, the influential politician, professor or expert usually has an easy escape from the responsibility to explain a statement, from a fundamental responsibility to the public as a person whose opinion carries considerable weight. Insisting on answers is poor manners. It is generally considered more important to observe The Rules than to understand what influential people are telling us. In fact, The Rules are used as an excuse for not getting explanations, not getting any understanding of what an influential person is saying. There is little expressed concern over how costly it is for our system to fail to get clear on the directions we are taking in our domestic and foreign policy. Nobody questions The Rules.

Occasionally there are public discussions which may appear to discard The Rules and offer genuine give and take. Debate is sometimes offered to the public as a means of evaluating domestic and foreign policies of the United States. But real debate is generally presented in a courtroom or sports arena atmosphere not conducive to careful evaluation of ideas. Participants tend to engage in a contest to score points or humiliate or discredit an opponent. Coming out on top usually takes precedence over evaluating ideas. At the other extreme, as many as eight people can be seen in a television "debate" which is essentially a monologue. All are in basic agreement except for emphasis or details. In either case, obvious if awkward questions are either trampled in the scuffle for advantage or are politely avoided. Even in a "heated exchange" certain rules are rarely violated. After the dust has settled, it generally turns out that it was all done in rather careful observance of The Rules.

For all the promotional superlatives over televised "debates" and "confrontations," there are few dialogues on domestic and foreign policy in which any serious challenge is made to what someone wants to believe. This would be bad form, against The Rules. There are few discussions in which there is true interaction between a person supporting an idea and a questioner testing it for consistency with reported facts. We are far more likely to get the same old shopworn slogans and arguments.

If some brave soul should venture to break The Rules, there could be genuine discussion, genuine evaluation of ideas, opinions and slogans. The public would finally have a chance to understand statements endlessly repeated without explanation. But the professors, politicians and experts prefer to stick to their habits, not getting directly involved with each other or with the public. It is easier and safer to write books, articles or columns or give lectures or speeches in circumstances where questioning is, or can be made to be, limited or superficial. All this is easier than having to ask or answer questions or explain one's own ideas and opinions in the light of news reports.

The Rules successfully suppress dialogue. Public dialogue is restricted where it is most needed. Whether The Rules were formed and perpetuated out of fear, superstition or laziness, the effect is to make things easier and safer, in the short run, for the influential people. It permits them the luxury of taking the path of least resistance.

*   *   *

Each society is blessed or burdened with its guiding assumptions and resulting policies which determine actions it will take. In many societies, the official guiding assumptions and policies must be and will be followed without question. There is virtually no choice.

In the United States we have a choice as to which guiding assumptions we will adopt, which policies we will follow. We also have a choice as to how we will evaluate and select policies and assumptions. One alternative is to accept and rely on opinions which result in assumptions and policies because the opinions have been examined and explained, because they have been discussed, evaluated and reconciled with reported facts. The other alternative is to accept and rely on opinions which result in guiding assumptions and policies merely because opinions are repeated by influential people until they are widely believed, whether or not they have ever been explained. We like to think this is something that happens only in "other countries," that it doesn't happen here.

Where there is political freedom, the question of whether opinions and guiding assumptions will be discussed and evaluated or merely repeated until they seem valid is largely up to the influential people of that society. The politicians, professors, officials and experts in the U.S. have decided there will be no public discussion of certain ideas and opinions, even though it would be permitted under our laws. The influential people have demonstrated an aversion to discussing in public, among themselves, certain issues they are perfectly willing to write about. The result is that we have in the U.S. a bland, comfortable monologue method of evaluating certain ideas and assumptions, including those bearing on the most sensitive issues of domestic and foreign policy.

The monologue method of evaluating ideas, imposed by The Rules, envisions that opinions will be set forth in books, magazines, newspaper columns and in broadcast media but under no circumstances will the influential people publicly

4

discuss these opinions among themselves. The public has access to information, the reported facts appearing in news media. The public also has access to opinion, which includes intrepretations as to the meaning of facts as seen by the influential people. But it is strictly against The Rules for two influential people, two professors, politicians, experts, officials or columnists, to have public discussion on differing opinions derived from the same reported facts to see which opinion is more readily supported by facts. There is no law prohibiting such discussion. It is simply against The Rules which decree that a safe, easy monologue method of evaluating ideas shall prevail in the United States.

Opinions and ideas which have flourished under the monologue system include the assumption that there can be "détente" between the U.S. and Russia, that trade will lead to better relations between the two countries and that the U.S. is implicitly to blame for any residual tensions because of its insistence on restricting trade and credits to the Soviet Union. These opinions have been repeated by influential people. We all know this is very easily done. But for all the public discussion among people of opposing views, one would think many of the widely accepted opinions to be self-evident truths, settled beyond the need for any discussion in public, settled beyond any question. Apparently no discussion is considered necessary to see whether these opinions, or the opposing views, can be reconciled with the many available and pertinent reported facts.

Unfortunately, most of the opinion as to the meaning of reported facts is presented in the monologue mode, generally in written form. There are many reported facts which appear to the layman to be at variance with the notion of "détente" between the U.S. and Russia. It is very easy to get the impression that there is little evidence that the Soviet Union is interested in any genuine, lasting relaxation of tensions. But it is quite possible that reported facts could be reconciled with the idea of relaxed tensions if a proponent of the opinion would answer questions about it. Unfortunately, it looks as if we will never know because it looks as if no one is going

5

to ask one of the influential people to answer questions on television, at a university or in a lecture hall so the results of the discussion could be made known to the public.

What we have in this country is a monologue system for manufacturing opinions, for evaluating ideas, for deciding on guiding assumptions, for determining the meaning of the continuous flow of news reports. As a result, influential people have learned they can say nearly anything they want to, and repeat it as often as they want to, no matter how seemingly oblivious of reported facts, without having to worry that someone may ask them to explain statements in terms of reports. If asked, the question will be asked in accordance with The Rules, in a written form which is easy to ignore or evade, easy to denounce as "unworthy of reply" with no further explanation.

*   *   *

Why do we need discussion of opinion? Why do we need to violate The Rules, to get away from easy, safe monologue? The influential people seem to think all we need is information in the form of news and the opinions of the influential people. From these, it seems, the public is supposed to decide which opinions and policies to support, as policies are often based on opinion. The long-standing opinion that "détente" was effective and valid as a concept thus became the policy of pursuing the goal of détente between the U.S. and Russia.

The influential people apparently believe that the public doesn't need or deserve discussion involving the evaluation or questioning of different opinions. If a prominent State Department official gives various reasons for his opinion favoring détente and if a prominent U.S. Senator gives various reasons for opposing détente, or a certain version of it, the public is supposed to have no difficulty choosing which opinion, and which policy, to support by means of the ballot, the opinion poll, letters or other political leverage. When experts disagree, and refuse to discuss their disagreement, the public is supposed to have no difficulty determining whose opinion is more easily supported by the pertinent facts.

The public is continually confronted with equally respected influential people forming opposite opinions on what is presumably the same set of reported facts. In many cases it is difficult to say that these opposing views are equally valid or that "the truth lies somewhere between." What is missing in our political experience is discussion aimed at evaluating ideas.

As a result of the lack of public dialogue the public is cheated out of the benefits of discussion, out of the presentation of two views in close sequence so an evaluation can be made. We need public discussion because the public has little opportunity to prepare to make a sound judgment as to whether some of the tempting, comfortable slogans can really be explained in terms of reported facts. The professors, politicians and experts may worry that their favorite slogans can't stand questioning or that the public may begin to think independently of the familiar, comfortable assumptions if it appears they can't be explained. Perhaps they are unwilling to take the chance.

Yet the public may have to decide whether to endorse policies such as "détente" in elections and may have to suffer adverse consequences of supporting policies which were often repeated and rarely examined. Under our system, it is difficult for the public to avoid making some sort of choice, deliberately or by default, as respects the support or non-support of opinion and resulting policy. It is equally difficult to avoid unpleasant consequences of policies which were adopted merely on the basis of repetition in the complete absence of awkward questions. This is why we need public discussion. When influential people refuse to take part in public discussion of policy, the public gets only two of the three items needed to form judgments, only raw information and untested opinion. Very few influential opinions have been examined in discussion involving simple, obvious, necessary questions.

We need public discussion because without a process of testing by people who are familiar with pertinent information and can effectively marshal reported facts, the public may have great difficulty finding a basis for assessment and

7

reaching the duly considered conclusions our system demands of us. Scholars, experts and journalists often recall and apply information which tends to become lost during the repetition of slogans.

Assumptions regarding détente, trade, responsibility for the cold war, interference in the internal affairs of other countries, could be decisive. If we are being told that certain policies are "wrong" for the United States when they may be necessary to protect our interests, we obviously may fail to protect our interests. This is not to say which policies are actually justified and which are not, but only to say that we shouldn't make such decisions without extensive public discussion to evaluate ideas. The U.S. voting and opinion-polling public's acceptance or rejection of certain national efforts has carried great weight in our very recent past. Public acceptance or rejection of certain assumptions about national interests could be pivotal in the question of whether the U.S. and the Western allies manage to hold firm against opposing pressures.

*   *   *

The monologue method of evaluating ideas is well-suited to the Soviet political system. Although information and opinion are plentiful in Russia, the variety is limited and there is "unanimous" agreement that no discussion of official opinions or policies is "necessary." It is quite appropriate and compatible with the Soviet system that opinions are formed in a vacuum, without dissent, debate or discussion. Critical comment from the public, from outside the Communist ruling elite, is suppressed. While a greater variety of opinion is permitted in the U.S., there is still the question of whether our political system contemplates that decisions will be made in a vacuum, without public testing and questioning to see whether they can be explained.

The idea that trade will lead to better relations has had official sanction in both the U.S. and Russia. It was understandable that in 1975 no one in Russia except Andre Sakharov was questioning this but what was the excuse in this country? We are free to challenge official slogans in public discussion. If we fail to use what we have going for us, what can we expect for the future?

The influential people write. They speak. But they don't converse. Where is the dialogue, the interaction between people of opposing views? As a practical matter, people in the U.S. or U.S.S.R. tend to accept ideas and assumptions that pass without question. As a practical matter, we evaluate and accept ideas here much as it is done in Russia, on the basis of the monologue method, according to The Rules. Occasionally there may in the U.S. be some explanation or some discussion but most ideas and assumptions are accepted whether or not questions about them have been asked or answered satisfactorily by any standard. If we really believe issues such as détente, trade and responsibility for tensions are settled beyond the need for questions and answers, beyond any need for public discussion, we are in deep trouble. We are hopelessly locked in to the monologue system. We have chosen, by default, not to test and evaluate what at any moment may be or may become a guiding assumption governing domestic and foreign policy.

We therefore have no idea what the possibilities are, what changes might result from discussion and involvement of the leading thinkers and the general public in the process of evaluating ideas. If public opinion favors "détente" at a particular time, would opinion be the same if the obvious questions had been asked and answered? If we form and follow détente policies without discussion, the result could be as unpleasant as the result of forming Vietnam policies based on slogans. If we make errors on détente, will they necessarily be any less serious than whatever errors were made on Vietnam? They could be much more serious.

The professors, politicians and experts have clung to the monologue method of evaluating ideas and forming opinions. They have clung to their slogans, doctrines and dogmas and left their countrymen to decide the most deeply serious matters of national policy without the benefit of hearing questions and answers as to whether doctrines and news reports can be made compatible. If these people are willing to put ideas in print, why not explain them? If they are willing to write about difficult, sensitive issues, why not talk about them?

The professors, politicians, experts and officials have a good thing going. They can write freely about their opinions without having to worry about reported facts which may interfere with what they have decided to believe. They don't have to worry about saying to each other in discussion what they may say to each other in print. They can write about sensitive issues without having to get involved in the difficult, risky business of discussing them. In Russia, men and women risk their lives attempting to restore the rights that simply go to waste in the United States.

Were it not for The Rules, we could talk about whether the monologue method of evaluating ideas is compatible with our political system. Perhaps our system requires that decisions be made on the basis of challenge, question and dialogue to stimulate thought rather than on the basis of slogans which may be substitutes for thought. Dialogue has valuable advantages over monologue. For example, reported facts conveniently ignored by one party can be politely restored by the other to preserve a more balanced view, to maintain a spirit of inquiry, both of which are forbidden in Russia. Neither monologue nor dialogue is by itself sufficient; we need both opinion and the discussion of opinion. Apparently it is almost as unthinkable here as it is in Russia that an influential person should go on television with a politician, government official, or someone who can represent official views, to get explanations of "détente" in the light of reported facts, or for an opponent of détente to explain the reasons for opposition.

The monologue method makes us act too much like Russians. There is little point in having a variety of information and opinion if we don't discuss and evaluate contending ideas in the light of what everybody knows. The influential people maintain their silence. For all the public discussion of whether détente and trade will lead to better relations between the U.S. and Russia, whether these ideas can be reconciled with reports, we might as well be Russians.

Selling computers reported to have potential for military use, selling them to the Soviet Union may be the best thing or the worst thing we could do, or somewhere in between. But no one wants to start public discussion on which it may be. Dead silence. Apparently it is considered to concern only those manufacturers doing business with the Soviet Government. But what about the rest of us? Is it really none of our business? Why not ask? What are we afraid of?

*   *   *

The result of the easy way is that we seem to be drifting on slogans instead of steering our course by evaluating ideas. The slogans mentioned are just a few of many. The long-term policies of the country are too important to be determined by slogans which may be substitutes for thinking. On one hand we have a tremendous educational task and on the other hand a great informing and potentially educating national resource in virtually every living room. But we refuse to use it for the benefit of our society and government. Our civilization may end not with a bang or a whimper but with a quiz show or a cat food commercial.

We need questions on trade, "détente" and other matters to make us think, to offset reassuring slogans which may try to persuade us not to think. Our system was never intended to flourish or even sustain itself under a blanket of timid silence.

Without discussion of opinion, there is no way of knowing which opinions are accepted because they can be explained and which are accepted merely through persistent repetition. Should we attempt to distinguish between the two? Without knowing which ideas can be explained, there is no way of knowing the extent to which the country is being run by slogans, which may be substitutes for thinking. The influential people are nevertheless determined not to end their preening, scolding self-centered soliloquies and to start putting their opinions on the line for questioning.

There is evidence that we fail to ask simple, obvious questions simply for fear of offending influential people. In the January 4, 1976 issue of *The New York Times,* television critic John J. O'Connor commented as follows:

> . . . Most (television) panel formats are carefully designed to protect the interests of the guest. When questions are rotated among a group of journalists, the results are virtually guaranteed to be superficial. A questioner getting close to the core of one subject will find that his time is up. Another questioner takes over and, more often than not, begins to pursue an entirely different subject. The reason for this standard routine is purely practical. Without some built-in image safeguards, prominent politicians, the kind most courted for television, would simply refuse to appear on panel shows. The appeal of vanity may be strong, but the fear of genuine confrontation is stronger.
>
> While the politician works mightily toward "positive projections," the correspondent faces the danger of creating negative vibrations for himself merely by standing still. With the politician smiling broadly and appearing thoroughly reasonable, the correspondent venturing to ask normally tough questions may find himself the victim of a distorted image. Consider the case of CBS's Dan Rather, who, during the scandalous Watergate scenario, had the temerity not to back off from questioning Richard Nixon. The questions were not exceptionally incisive, but the mere asking of them suggested an unusual confrontation and transformed Mr. Rather, a relatively pleasant type, into either folk hero or a biased villain, depending on the political persuasion of the judges. . . .

If Mr. O'Connor is correct, it means we are required to be afraid to get clear on opinions, assumptions and issues for fear of offending the touchy egos of the influential people. It is not only from members of the press that influential people expect this same courtesy, this diplomatic immunity among their own countrymen. It is also a professional courtesy among influential people themselves to allow colleagues to say whatever they want to say without asking them directly and publicly to account for it.

The implications of Mr. O'Connor's remarks are appalling. The influential person is under no circumstances to be obliged to explain what he says. Everyone must understand and accept the possibility that the influential person may be refusing to explain what he says because he himself doesn't understand what he says. We are to accept what the influential person says, whether he understands it, whether he can explain it or not. The influential person, who is deciding on the basis of his opinions what guiding assumptions and policies our society and government will rely on, may or may not understand those opinions and anyone who asks whether he understands them is considered to be guilty of sheer impudence. This is one of the effects of the monologue system, The Rules, the easy way of evaluating ideas.

The political atmosphere in the U.S. is not the suffocating repression of Russia. But in many ways the silence here is dreadfully similar to the silence of Russia.

The influential people in the U.S. are giving the American public the silent treatment. Some merely proclaim that trade will lead to better relations with Russia. Never mind any loose ends or nagging questions as to whether Russia *wants* better relations with the U.S. or even whether their system based on suspicion can afford better relations with the West in any way that will benefit anyone except the small ruling elite in Russia. Never mind the persistent reports that any easing of tensions, any slackening in the ideological struggle is regarded by Soviet officials as a threat of enormous proportions calling for immediate corrective action. There are to be no better relations in any meaningful sense of confidence and understanding among peoples; there is to be no talk of persons and information crossing borders. Hatred and suspicion are to be protected and preserved at all costs.

"I'm aware of this and so are you," the influential person seems to say, "but if it doesn't bother me it shouldn't bother you so I'm not going to explain why I think trade will change this." The public has been hearing for years that the

13

Soviet system must as a matter of policy play Soviet peoples off against other peoples as "enemies" in order to instill fear and impose discipline, in order to survive, and that Russians themselves can't trust the ruling elite, the Party members, the five per cent of the people who run Russia. But some influential people would have us believe trade is going to "open contacts" and change all that and the average citizen is supposed to understand perfectly.

If the influential people mean "better relations" only with the ruling elite in Russia, they should say so and mention that these "good relations" can be, and have been, turned on and off like an electric light. If they mean "good relations" with "the Russians," with the other 95%, a lessening of suspicion and isolation, they should explain that also. There may be perfectly satisfactory answers to the obvious questions or there may be counterbalancing considerations based on reported facts. But the influential people are seeing to it that there is no public discussion among themselves on these questions. We are simply going to drift on slogans.

The influential person seems to say, "Here is my statement. It may conflict with statements others have made. It may conflict with statements I have made. It may seem to be in head-on collision with information available from any newspaper. But I have spoken and that should be enough; accept it without explanation."

Apparently this situation is so "normal" it doesn't bother the influential people that their colleagues make statements which have not been explained and which seem to leave simple, obvious questions unanswered. In deference to their fellows, they are willing to leave unresolved those gaping differences between apparently incompatible opinions and news reports. Perhaps the differences can be reconciled but the politicians and professors are seeing to it that we will never know. They seem content to leave themselves and everyone else confused or uncertain as to how ideas and reports can be reconciled, carefully avoiding the obvious questions that thrust themselves forward.

No doubt the influential people would be offended if asked

whether this is real intellectual leadership or just laziness and sloppy thinking.

* * *

Many influential people have expressed concern that things are going badly for us in the United States, as if it were difficult to understand. Perhaps it is not really amazing that things are going badly. Perhaps it is more amazing that we are still here, as a united and independent country.

What can we reasonably expect when we are afraid to ask people who make domestic and foreign policy to explain what they say? Should we wonder that things don't go right? As long as we permit the influential people to act like foreign ambassadors with diplomatic immunity from difficult questions, we can't expect things to get better.

We have a choice. We can steer our course by discussing and evaluating ideas we use to develop national policy or we can choose to drift aimlessly on the slogans which are most often repeated, because they are often repeated, not because they have been tested in public discussion. Generally speaking, the influential people in the United States have made a choice that we will drift on slogans. Whether a choice is made deliberately or by default, the consequences are the same. As long as we drift, things will tend to go badly.

It may be safe to predict that things will go badly as long as the influential people hide out from the public and from each other. It may take some prodding from the public to get influential people to ask each other what they are doing and saying. If the influential people and the general public fail to see that this is done, we all deserve whatever we get for permitting this criminal negligence. By allowing ourselves to drift on a sea of untested slogans, we are committing a crime against our system, a crime for which we must expect penalties to be imposed sooner or later. Drifting on slogans isn't what the founders of the republic had in mind. The system they devised will not sustain itself if we drift on slogans. If the influential people won't willingly accept their responsibilities in our society, the general public will have

15

to do what it can to talk, persuade, pressure or shame them into it.

The general public may have to demonstrate, protest, picket, boycott and use leverage against the influential people to get them to face their responsibilities. It may take pressure to get them to accept their obligations to our system. It may take persuasion to get them to consider what they owe their society and government in return for their privileges, rewards and fringe benefits. Their manicured soliloquies aren't sufficient to sustain our system. Their monologues represent only half their responsibility.

If there were open discussion, we might find that The Rules are keeping us from using our resources. If use of a system's resources is necessary to maintain the system, The Rules could mean trouble. Are The Rules causing us to use our communications resources as if we had some other kind of system, in which open discussion is forbidden? Can the flabbiness of our system be traced to lack of use, to the fears and hangups of the influential people? We may be wasting the best part of our freedom, freedom of speech, but the influential people don't want any public discussion about *that*. Obviously it would be against The Rules to discuss The Rules.

The Rules may have put us in the difficult position of trying to manage an important responsibility without full input, without being involved in discussion of the full range of ideas and options relative to a given problem. A corporation or university officer would certainly balk at having to make decisions under these conditions. But U.S. voters do it all the time. We would never try to run a public relations firm or a college according to The Rules. But this is the way we are trying to run the country. It is obvious to many people that things aren't going well in the United States. But how can it be a healthy state of affairs when no influential person ever has to explain anything he says? There must always be an escape from what would seem the fundamental responsibility to clarify or explain one's own statements.

If some say the U.S. is in trouble, we shouldn't wonder. We

live in a world where political doctrines and systems are in serious competition. Although we don't admire the methods, other countries exploit all the advantages in competition which their systems afford. We may have to become as willing to use our system as we are to defend it with billions for weapons. It would be ironic indeed if our demise should result from internal stagnation imposed by intellectual timidity, by The Rules, rather than from some widely advertised combination of external threats. We could lose to competition or we could collapse in our own inertia.

The success of our system may depend on whether we can turn away from the easy pleasure of escape to the demanding satisfaction of involvement, at least occasionally. Our system demands involvement even as The Rules forbid it. We can't indefinitely draw on our inheritance, on what our forbears built and defended. If we are to remain politically solvent we will have to contribute some effort of our own.

If our institutions and businesses are worth preserving, and if they need our social and political climate to survive, we will have to consider giving at least some effort to discussion of national policy. There ought to be some television time left in between the quiz shows and cat food commercials. The question everyone is avoiding is the question of whether our actions show that we consider our social and political system as worthy of preservation as our other institutions and our businesses. Our actions may show an underlying assumption that almost everything *except* government requires our attention and involvement. This is the assumption which manifests itself in The Rules. It could be a costly assumption. We ought to talk about it.

2

Détente Between the United States and Russia

"There is now détente between the U.S. and Russia" is an example of an idea that is often mentioned but rarely discussed publicly with the aim of reconciling it with reported facts. From statements of advocates and opponents of the idea, it may be difficult for the interested observer to form a clear impression of what "détente" means.

Terms often used to describe or define détente are "relaxation," "lessening of tensions" and "movement away from confrontation," to list a few. It is also described as an arrangement under which "competition" or "ideological struggle" will continue but with certain rules and safeguards to avoid "war," meaning certain kinds of war. The terms which are used tend to convey an impression of moving away from what is negative or undesirable and are not necessarily coupled with the idea or moving toward what is positive and desirable. When a positive hoped-for benefit is mentioned, it usually amounts to something like "cooperation."

No two people will agree as to what is meant by détente but for the sake of an arbitrary starting place let us say that one goal of détente should be to move away from fear, tension and confrontation and, if possible, toward confidence and cooperation.

Was there any comprehensive public discussion as to what we should reasonably have expected from détente? Were we hoping to change Soviet foreign policy? Were we hoping to reduce the danger of nuclear war? Were we hoping détente would help us avoid conflicts involving only conventional weapons? Were our hopes in any of these categories for the long term or for the short term only? To what extent were our expectations realized? There is little evidence of any public discussion aimed at comparing our expectations with reported facts which indicate the actual results. It may therefore be difficult to know what policy to pursue in the future. Without looking back, we lack guidance for the future.

During his 1974 visit to Moscow, President Nixon declared that the U.S. and Russia were moving away from confrontation and in the direction of negotiations, even learning cooperation.

Regardless of one's definition of détente, it was probably expected, on the U.S. side, that there would be not only an easing of tensions in direct relationships between the U.S. and Russia but also a slackening of pressure in various potential trouble spots in other parts of the world. Statements of U.S. officials concerning Vietnam and Angola seemed to indicate the U.S. expected a relenting in "proxy" confrontations as well as direct confrontations.

The U.S. evidently expected that the Soviet Union would scale down aid to North Vietnam and would not be so eager to inject its weapons and supplies into sensitive areas such as Angola. The United States Government seems to have expected that détente would also help insure the two powers against "indirect" conflicts such as the Middle East, in which armed forces of Russia and the U.S. might have found themselves in "direct" confrontation, according to news reports.

It later appeared that few of these expectations were justified and that many assumptions were incorrect.

Following reports of intervention by outside forces in Angola, some relevant questions appeared in a December 17, 1975 *New York Times* editorial:

(The pertinent text is in *italics* supplied by the author. *The New York Times* requires that when its editorials

19

are reprinted, they be reprinted in their entirety.)

The essentials of the Soviet, Cuban and American involvement in Angola have finally become public knowledge. The crucial need now is to arrive at a sensible policy.

Secretary Kissinger has argued that financial and arms aid to the factions fighting the Soviet-back Popular Movement for the Liberation of Angola (MPLA) is needed to achieve a military stalemate and prepare the ground for a negotiated settlement. Whether the aid is covert, or whether it is open—as in Vietnam from the beginning in the 1950's—the danger of being dragged into another Vietnam war is feared by many.

Yesterday, Administration officials sought to allay this fear by reporting that President Ford had ruled out any intervention by American troops or advisers. But the question remains: *What steps must be taken to assure that Angola does not become another Vietnam? Does this require cutting off all financial and arms aid? Or does it merely entail keeping American personnel out of the combat area? The Congress should address this question today, not just the technical matter of whether any C.I.A. funds in the defense budget can be used in Angola.*

Furthermore, Congressional discussion is needed on what, if any, measures the country is prepared to take to discourage the intervention of the Soviet Union and some 4,000 Cuban troops in this African civil war. What about the impact on detente? Should the United States be shipping grain to Russia in the face of such lawless behavior? Why has not the United States—or one or more African states—indicted the Soviet and Cuban intervention before the Security Council? West Europe and the United States undoubtedly can bring non-military pressure to bear upon the situation. There is every reason to move vigorously in this direction.

Both the White House and the Congress ought also clear up their own administrative confusion. Eight Congressional subcommittees were allegedly briefed last summer and some of them were evidently informed again within recent days of covert Administration activities, as required by last year's amendment to the foreign aid act. Yet the Speaker of the House stated this week that he had not been informed and Senator Mansfield, the majority leader, who heads one of the eight committees briefed by the Administration, has implied lack of knowledge as well.

It is evident that the Congress should create a single, responsible joint committee, similar to the Joint Atomic Energy Committee, that can act for the Congress in overseeing intelligence and covert operations. As for Angola, the Congress as a whole is at least in a position to assume a joint responsibility with the Administration for American policy there. The first task is to shape a policy, then to see that it is carried out.

Any of these questions, or numerous other questions which were also raised, could have served as a basis for public discussion. As usual, there was silence.

The repeated statements that there is or should be détente, that it is some sort of continuing process which requires new agreements, should mean we can expect some movement away from confrontation toward cooperation. If we are told that these expectations are too high, that we are lucky to have enough détente so we can have peace, so we can stay alive, détente may be difficult for some people to distinguish from the bad old days of the "cold war." It has been pointed out that we did manage to remain alive and independent during the "cold war confrontation" whenever this was supposed to have ended. If a movement from confrontation to some form of cooperation is too much to expect from détente, it is difficult to see what we have gained from it, in fact difficult to see what has changed from "cold war" days. There are among the influential in the U.S. enthusiastic supporters and hard-line critics of détente or of the particular kind of détente the U.S. may have pursued at one time or another. But will they get together for a public discussion of their views, hopes and differences? Not a word.

In spite of discouraging reports there apparently are at least some people who hope that détente can lead to con-

21

fidence and cooperation which may grow out of a gradual "mellowing" of the Soviet Union as we draw "the Russians" into agreements, gain their confidence and establish commercial relationships they might be reluctant to damage by certain forms of unpleasantness, such as a return to "cold war" tactics.

It might be helpful if the political leaders and commentators would publicly discuss among themselves what we can reasonably expect from détente. Has the Soviet Union changed any internal or external policies since the supposed advent of détente around 1972? Has the Soviet Union been avoiding actions, in various parts of the world, which could lead to confrontation? How often are questions such as these asked and answered on television or in some other medium readily accessible to the public?

It is probably quite true that we can never expect any agreement on questions such as these. But is that any reason for not discussing them? Even if we can never entirely agree, discussion may produce an educational experience and a resulting consensus which didn't previously exist. People might have bases for judgment which they didn't previously have. The politicians and professors rarely hesitate to write about détente or talk about détente in the monologue mode. But they seem to be united and determined not to have any discussion about it with influential people of differing or opposing views. They seem determined not to put their views alongside reported facts and allow themselves to be questioned as to any possible discrepancies.

In shipping quantities of arms to various trouble spots in addition to arming itself to the teeth, the Soviet Union raises the question of whether it has accepted the "cooperation" or even the "coexistence" theory of détente. The question as to what has changed, what there is about the "current détente" that separates it from "peaceful coexistence" is one that the experts refuse to discuss for the benefit of the public. When did détente begin? What happened to mark its beginning? What subsequent events served to maintain its progress? How has the pattern of Soviet actions changed? These are some of the questions that seem to suggest themselves and seem to deserve answers.

The questions which have not been asked or answered seem rather simple and obvious. If there is no terrifying, cliffhanging confrontation between the U.S. and U.S.S.R. at a particular moment, it certainly appears that they are preparing for a confrontation with somebody. It is consistently reported that Russia is building, or has the capacity to build, two or three times as many conventionally powered submarines as the U.S. Its tank production may be even more disproportionate. Estimates of tank production vary from five to ten times as many as the U.S. produces. Leaving land-based and sea-based nuclear weapons aside for the moment, what are the possible peaceful uses of a tank or of a submarine, even a submarine with conventional power or conventional weapons? Why is Russia building these generally offensive weapons if it doesn't plan to exploit them, to use them or threaten to use them sooner or later? If there is détente at the moment, are the Soviets planning for détente in the future?

Perhaps it can be argued that the vast array of Soviet armor in Eastern Europe is more of a threat to China than to NATO. Perhaps it can be argued that the submarines Russia is building are more of a threat to China than to Japan, Europe or the U.S. There may be many reasons to assume that Russia is in imminent danger of attack from NATO or from China, that any conflicts Russia may have with NATO, Japan or China will not be of Russian origin. Much is made of the Chinese threat to Russia but where are the reasons for assuming China plans to attack a power with such awesome retaliatory capacity? Perhaps it is all perfectly reasonable but the foreign policy experts are very carefully avoiding any public discussion of any of the questions which seem to suggest themselves.

There may not be clearcut answers on any of these issues. There may not be satisfactory answers or any answers at all. But the influential people are making sure that the general public will never know. By avoiding public discussion they are seeing to it that the general public does not have the basis it needs to make the judgments it may be called on to make under the system of government we have.

Perhaps the answers to the questions raised here are readily available. Perhaps there are counterbalancing considerations that nullify the questions. Perhaps there are other questions which would cancel them out. Perhaps there are reasons why the questions are unfair. There may be reasons why the questions should not be asked in the first place. But the conscientious, reasonably well-informed observer, the kind of person who may have to decide whether to endorse a policy for or against détente, under our system, simply may not know the answers.

For example, how can détente be reconciled with intense, daily, virulent anti-West propaganda that is heaped on the Soviet populace? Is this constant psychological conditioning to fear and hatred conducive to cooperation or even coexistence? Everyone who follows the news is aware of these reports. Everyone who follows the news is aware of the talk about détente. Are the two compatible? Judging by the amount of public discussion on these questions, it appears as if at least some of the influential people would rather not know.

There are persistent reports that the Soviet Union continues to accumulate conventional military capability of a kind not usually associated with defense (submarines of the conventional type, for example), still seeks the demise of NATO and the domination of Western Europe, still refuses onsite verification of mutual troop reduction, weapons testing and disarmament, using verification methods acceptable to other countries. There are reports that the Soviet Government considers all uncensored information, not just "Western ideas" to be subversive. There are reports of an artificially induced fundamental hostility toward other societies, reports that Soviets are pressing doctrines of class struggle and mandatory conflict with other societies as necessary and inevitable, all of which may be verified simply by reading translated items from *Pravda*. What has changed?

The signs point to maintenance by the Soviet Union of thought-control and minority rule, of continued isolation, confinement and xenophobia of the Soviet populace. Apparently the Soviet Government intends not only to keep the barbed wire, mine fields, censorship and artificial hatred, but to keep the need for these barriers.

Can there be détente representing the slightest change if the Soviet people are not allowed to inform themselves about the ideas and goals of other peoples? While there is isolation, can there be trust and understanding, a spirit of cooperation that should be the basis of détente? Understanding and confidence among peoples is not something that can be turned on and off at will by governments. If people are "enemies," they are easier to control by means of a system of minority rule. The Soviet Government has made it quite clear that it wants only the sort of détente that can be turned on and off like an electric light for the purposes of strategy, depending on the changing needs of ruling elite. Meanwhile, they frantically build weapons in preparation for a confrontation with somebody.

Discussion might indicate that many of these questions are invalid. Discussion might demonstrate that they have been answered or that they can be answered. Discussion might reveal other questions which, in effect, are answers to those indicated above. Any number of things might happen if there were discussion, if people had to deal with reported facts they might prefer not to deal with. But the leading thinkers in domestic and foreign policy are seeing to it that there is no public dialogue, no educational process involving influential people and the public, only silence.

Raising questions about détente and related matters in no way demonstrates that the talk of détente is invalid or that we have in any way been deceived about détente. This is only to say that there are certain reported facts which appear to a layman observer to be in conflict with the idea of détente and the manner in which it is used and generally understood. The reported facts may be inconsistent with the idea or may only appear to be. But when asked what has really changed from the days of the "cold war," someone lacking in expertise may not know.

There are those who say that during the cold war we were not giving the Soviet Union massive injections of badly needed food, credits and technology. During the cold war years we weren't shipping them computers of a type they have not produced for themselves and which can be used to perfect MIRV missile systems for eventual exploitation against somebody. If Russia was building weapons at a rate equal to ours during the cold war days and is now building them at a rate exceeding ours, perhaps we were better off when they were doing it on their own without our valuable assistance. If the Russians are so confident in their predictions that they will triumph over us in one way or another, they ought to be able to manage it without our help. Is there any validity in these views? None of the influential thinkers in the U.S. is willing to talk about it publicly, to exchange views.

To some people it is difficult to reconcile the idea of détente with reported facts. Others may insist that there is nothing in news reports in recent years to indicate there is any cold war left, to indicate any tensions, conflicts, confrontations resulting from divergent purposes of the U.S. and Russia. They may be able to marshall as many reported facts in favor of the idea as others have gathered to question the idea. What is missing is any direct contact, any conversation between those who claim reported facts support détente and those who claim that events clearly show there is no détente.

To a layman, the lack of public discussion is mystifying. Perhaps those who believe there is no détente are afraid that this belief can't be reconciled with reported facts or, as the saying goes, they "have made up their minds." Perhaps they are afraid they might have to change their minds if certain reports, other than those which militate against détente, were introduced in the form of questions.

Those who favor détente seem to have the same fear of

direct contact with those who oppose détente and the facts available to the opponents to justify their opposition. Perhaps the proponents of détente want to avoid having reported facts imposed on them in the form of direct questions. In this situation, they must attempt to discredit a reported fact, must reconcile it with the idea of détente or must alter their viewpoint to some degree. All of these options can be awkward and uncomfortable.

Regardless of whether one is politically "liberal" or "conservative," what we may be seeing is an intellectual conservatism in the sense of wanting to "hang on" to favored ideas and slogans. People who are aware of reported facts which are antagonistic to what they want to believe seem to avoid confrontation with the reported facts.

Some experts in the U.S. may insist that détente means no more than a continued balance of terror, a continued coexistence, that it was never reasonable to expect that it would lead to cooperation between the Western Alliance and the Soviet bloc. While this notion may satisfy many people in the U.S., Canada, Western Europe or Japan, the chances are that it will not be enough to satisfy the people of the Third World. Perhaps this is why the discussion of what we can and should expect from détente is perhaps more of a necessity than a luxury. What representatives of the poor people of the world think of détente and what their people get out of it may ultimately be more important than what NATO or the Warsaw Pact countries think of it.

If detente is to be limited to a "feeling" or a "spirit" or other atmospherics, it seems futile and insubstantial unless there can be some discernible result and unless that result involves a movement from confrontation toward cooperation.

Responsible individuals and agencies have estimated that one-quarter to one-third of the world's people are destitute by any standard. They are in constant need of food, housing or clothing which are generally considered "essential."

James Reston wrote in *The New York Times* of September 12, 1975, on efforts to control the arms race:

27

. . . [Secretary of State Kissinger is not likely] to make much progress with his new plan to help the poorest nations of the world so long as the total arms bill continues running at over $240 billion a year. These poor countries, with their soaring populations, have suffered the most as a result of continued worldwide inflation, the sudden rise in the cost of fuel, the deterioration of their terms of trade, and the prolonged recession in their export markets.

"Some 900 million people are now subsisting on incomes of less than $75 a year," Robert McNamara told the recent meeting of the World Bank here. "They are the absolute poor, living in situations so depraved as to be below any rational definition of human decency. . . ."

This is what the larger debate in Washington is all about, not merely ICBM's, cruise missiles and force levels. For Mr. Kissinger is arguing that poverty levels may be more of a threat to the security of the world than anything else, and that the startling disparity between the rich nations and the basket cases may be more important in the long run than the military disparity between the superpowers.

It seems nearly impossible that the needs of the desperately poor can be met while governments all over the world (and not just the governments of "powerful" or "rich" or "developed" countries) are spending such prodigious quantities of money and resources on military weapons. It is nearly inconceivable that the growing population of the globe will ever have adequate housing, clothing, nutrition and medical care while the arms race continues. The deprivation will continue while the great powers persist in confrontation and while the smaller powers imitate them or become involved as proxies because great powers don't want to square off directly against each other.

For this reason, any détente among small or large powers will be of very little value and have very little effect unless it produces a genuine movement toward cooperation, to the extent that it has a measurable effect in reducing the production of weapons. For this reason, any détente which does not show signs of producing such cooperation and confidence is basically wishful thinking, basically misleading, basically a sham. The genuine and durable solution to any of the problems of the destitute people of the world is going to require cooperation among governments. Any proposed solution which does not include such cooperation is a false promise and a cruel fraud.

It now appears that the human race has the intelligence and resources to solve the problems of providing adequate housing, food and clothing for most or perhaps all of the world's people. The land, the seas, the Earth appear to have adequate resources to provide, with some conditions, essential items even to a staggering 4 billion passengers. But there are conditions. One of these conditions is that there be cooperation among peoples. By extension, this means cooperation among governments.

Cooperation appears to be the missing element. We can talk of new sources of protein, new methods of housing construction, breakthroughs in medicine as means of improving the lot of the billion or so deprived people on this planet. We can hold out hope to those deprived of the dignity and enjoyment of their lives. But without the prospect of cooperation among governments, the promise is a hoax. The money will never be there; the materials will never be there. The means of transportation and distribution of what is needed will never be there until there is cooperation among governments and peoples. Cooperation is the human resource which is being withheld from the world's destitute. Unless détente (and not just between the U.S. and U.S.S.R.) produces cooperation, all of man's other efforts to produce enough to sustain a worthwhile and dignified life will very likely be in vain.

Perhaps it is not only a question of what professors, politicians, officials, experts and journalists think we should be getting from détente. The power of those who represent the destitute to disrupt business-as-usual between great powers increases each year. They may not have nearly as much

29

patience as great power leaders have. As their capacity to upset the balance of terror increases with the spread of nuclear weapons, so will their inclination to use the weapons, to use force. As the saying goes, "Beware of the man who has nothing to lose."

There are many other issues and questions which are of potential concern to those who are self-governing in the sense that they must endorse policies advanced by the leading social and political thinkers in a representative system. All of these are questions which should be of interest not just to laymen but to the influential people themselves, to see how their ideas will fare against the views of others and against comparison with reported facts. But what we are getting is either monologue or dead silence. There isn't even any discussion as to whether we can afford the risks involved.

The issue here is not whether there is détente or is no détente, nor whether there should be. The issue here is not whether we accept or reject a notion but whether we accept or reject it without discussion. The issue is whether opinions and slogans are passing as facts, whether we are accepting slogans as substitutes for thinking, whether we will monitor and control slogans or whether slogans will succeed in controlling our thinking.

If we are pursuing "confrontation for its own sake," we should change our policy. If we are "protecting our interests" within reasonable bounds, we should continue to do so.

The point is that we should at least talk about what we are doing. No one even wants to present public discussion based on the question of what we are doing now, much less what course we should set for the future. In order to set a course, a society or a ship's crew must know first where it is and second where it wants to go. Without knowing both, there can be no course, no purposeful direction. Without direction there can be only guesswork and drift. As long as we drift we play games with our form of government and our way of life.

3

Trade Between the United States and Russia

It has been said that "trade will lead to better relations between the U.S. and Russia," that it will dispel Soviet suspicions of the U.S., that it will build interrelations which will lead to conditions necessary for coexistence or perhaps even cooperation. Trade is often held out as the one light at the end of the tunnel, that light which beckons us away from confrontation and toward cooperation with the Soviet Union. The hope is that these better relations built on trade will lead to other benefits for both countries and for mankind. The end of the arms race is sometimes mentioned as an example.

Implicit in these views, however, is the assumption that the isolation and suspicion of the Soviet Union are due to the lack of more and better trade between the U.S. and Russia, that the fault or failure is somehow that of the U.S. The assumption is that the source of suspicion is external to the Soviet Union itself. There are reports, however, which do not seem to be in agreement with the assumption. For example, on September 23, 1973, the following article appeared in *The New York Times*:

A leading political scientist and historian says that the Soviet Union "is bound to be an unreliable partner" in East-West accommodation and cooperation.

Prof. Hans J. Morgenthau, Leonard Davis Distinguished Professor of Political Science at the City University of New York, writes in the October issue of the magazine The New Leader:

"A government that cuts itself and its people off from objective contact with the outside world, that becomes the prisoner of its own propaganda, cannot pursue a foreign policy one can rely on to recognize, let alone respect."

The Soviet Government, he says, "is bound to prove an unreliable partner in détente."

Professor Morgenthau, who has served as a consultant to the State and Defense Departments, refers to a recent book by Anatoly A. Gromyko, the son of Foreign Minister Andrei A. Gromyko and the head of the foreign policy section of the Soviet Academy of Science's Institute of the U.S.A. The book, the professor says, is a "frightening experience, it is a compendium of every nonsense ever uttered by Soviet propaganda about the United States.

"The nonsense permeates not only factual reporting and political interpretations but also moral judgment," Professor Morgenthau wrote. "The Soviet Union appears as the champion of all that is good in the world, especially peace, while the United States, bent on war, is the incarnation of evil.

"If the leaders of the Soviet Union believe the fictions Gromyko presents as facts—and there is no reason to assume they do not, since the American Institute is their main source of information about the U.S.—détente can be no more than a breathing spell in an ongoing struggle for total stakes.

"And it must be observed," Professor Morgenthau continues, "that primarily this breathing spell serves the interests of the Soviet Union, whom we are providing with economic and technical potential without any assurance of its ultimate uses. It is at this point that the character of the Soviet Government and its domestic policies become matters of vital relevance for the United States."

Another assumption implicit in the notion that "trade will lead to better relations between the U.S. and Russia" is that Russia wants better relations with the U.S. or with other Western countries. Some optimists conjure images of the Soviet ruling elite just waiting for the great day when there can be better relations between the U.S. and U.S.S.R.

However, there are some irksome, awkward reported facts which are difficult to reconcile with this notion. Even the casual reader of daily newspapers is aware that Soviet propaganda is directed primarily against the U.S. It is almost as if Russians need the United States as the official enemy of mankind for propaganda purposes, to scare their people into unquestioning cooperation with a system which isolates and confines them in a cocoon of thought-control and minority rule. In this sense, it might be difficult for them to get along without us. The thrust of this indoctrination is, "The Americans and their NATO henchmen are lurking out there waiting for the slightest excuse to pounce on Russia so you'd better cooperate with the Party and follow orders so we can work together to defend ourselves." If indoctrinated hatred and fear are essential components in a system of thought-control, it may not be correct to assume that a minority rule system will be eager to give up the control that maintains hatred and fear, in the name of "better relations," even for propaganda purposes.

The casual reader of the news has little trouble finding reported facts which seem incompatible with the notion that the Soviet ruling elite wants better relations, either between themselves and other governments or between their own people and the people of other countries. On October 1, 1973, the following article appeared in *The New York Times*:

> Moscow's small army of party propagandists, 100,000 strong, fanned out through the Soviet capital today to wage "aggressive, uncompromising" battle against Western ideas at a time of international détente.
>
> As the city's political indoctrination courses open their 1973-1974 school year tomorrow, lecturers were given detailed guidelines to be on the lookout for three inter-

related subversive trends among the Soviet populace.

A party directive described these trends as a tendency to take a "general human" rather than a narrowly Communist view of world events, a technocratic approach that threatened to erase East-West differences in this era of rapid scientific progress and apparent confusion about the difference between the cold war, now supposedly ended, and the continuing war of ideas, which is more alive than ever.

The instructions, addressed to political lecturers who spread the party line in a wide system of indoctrination courses, were contained in the Moscow city party newspaper, Moskovskaya Pravda. The author was Vladimir N. Yagodkin, city party secretary for ideology and propaganda. He was reported earlier this year to have defended the Kremlin's new policy toward the West on the ground that there is nothing wrong about signing a pact with the devil "if you are certain you can cheat the devil."

The party's political and economic lectures are offered after working hours at places of employment, in workers clubs and community centers, and in the so-called "red corners," or social rooms, of housing projects.

Mr. Yagodkin said 3.3 million Muscovites, or 45 per cent of the city's population, took such courses during the year. Similar indoctrination lectures are offered throughout the Soviet Union.

The particular stress this year, aimed at combating political misconceptions, appears to be the domestic counterpart of a Soviet propaganda effort directed at the West. The Government-controlled information media have made it plain that the Soviet Union will not give in to Western pressure to allow a freer flow of information and ideas. Western ideas are viewed as designed to undermine the Soviet system.

Mr. Yagodkin's instructions to political lecturers seemed to focus on a certain ideological confusion that may have arisen among ordinary citizens as the Kremlin avows a desire for an easing of tension in the political, economic and military spheres while remaining adamant in the realm of ideas.

The Moscow ideologist indicated that more and more

Soviet citizens might be taking the view that everyone on earth was part of one world and there was no longer any need for ideological confrontation.

"We are increasingly confronted with active attempts by bourgeois propaganda to suggest that the class-oriented (Communist) approach to social phenomena is one-sided and should be supplemented or replaced by an abstract 'general human' approach," Mr. Yagodkin said.

He rebutted this notion by quoting Lenin as having said that anyone who advocated such an outlandish non-political approach deserved to be "put in a cage and to be exhibited as if he were some sort of Australian kangaroo."

The indoctrination guidelines also pointed up the political perils of growing scientific and technical progress, as machine-oriented engineers and technicians, playing an increasingly important role in society, lose sight of ideological aspects.

"In this connection," Mr. Yagodkin said, "attention needs to be given to the threat of a technocratic approach to the solution of socio-economic problems."

He said the scientific and technical revolution required greater stress on the natural sciences and engineering and therefore posed a danger of detracting from political considerations.

The thorniest problem for political lecturers appeared to be a tendency among Soviet citizens to become ideologically lax now that the cold war was supposedly over.

"Propaganda workers must demonstrate, through reasoned argument, that there is no basis for equating ideological warfare with the cold war," Mr. Yagodkin said.

He said that the continuing ideological war was a "struggle of ideas between opposing social systems" while the cold war, which he said had been started by the West, sought to extend the war of ideas to relations between governments and to areas of politics, economics and military affairs.

Mr. Yagodkin did not explain why the contest of ideas ruled out a confrontation between Western ideas and Communist ideas within the Soviet Union. Party ideologists in the past have conceded that it would be an uneven struggle and that the influx of Western ideas would in effect "disarm" the Soviet Union ideologically.

Reports such as this raise the very fundamental question as to whether we are kidding ourselves in thinking trade will change these attitudes so there can be trust and understanding between the people or the governments of the U.S. and U.S.S.R. Some may argue that the best we can hope for is good relations between the two governments. But if the Soviet Government doesn't want good relations between Soviet and other peoples, to what extent can we trust the "good relations" which have been advocated by the Kremlin? For what benevolent or peaceful purpose do they want to keep the Soviet populace isolated, confined, fearful and hostile toward other peoples?

The casual reader of news reports may have a distinct problem with hearing about trade leading to the prospect of better relations and reading about items of news which seem difficult to reconcile with such optimism. The leading thinkers in foreign policy could be very helpful if they would publicly discuss these apparent difficulties. Perhaps they can demonstrate that there are no difficulties, that the expressed hopes for better relations and the news reports of obstacles to better relations are perfectly compatible if other ideas or other reported facts are introduced into consideration. But the layman who may be uncertain or confused is getting precious little help from the influential people, who may nevertheless expect the layman to support proposals for trade as a means of assuring peace.

The casual observer, lacking expertise, can easily form the impression that the whole Soviet doctrine of class struggle is totally dependent on "bad relations" with "enemies" such as the U.S. He may not see how we can reasonably expect to have "normal" or even "better" relations with a government which considers subversive such notions as "a general human approach" or an easing of tensions or an end to ideological warfare. Perhaps all these reports can be reconciled with hopes for a better relationship. Perhaps the apparent contradictions can be brushed aside with a few incisive questions, a few counterbalancing considerations or a few explanatory remarks. But the task of reconciling ideas with reports is one which the professors, politicians, intellectuals, experts and journalists seem reluctant to undertake on behalf of the general public. Instead, silence.

There is evidently the hope that trade will bring about an atmosphere of trust and cooperation between the U.S. and Russia. But there are persistent reports in readily accessible news sources that the Soviet peoples themselves cannot trust the Kremlin to abide by written documents such as the Soviet Constitution. Scholars who have compared the grant of rights in the Soviet Constitution with the grant of rights in the United States Constitution say there is practically no difference. There are also readily available reports that the Soviet peoples can't trust the Kremlin to respect basic rights and the principles of civilized conduct, such as allowing Valery Panov and his wife to leave the Soviet Union together, except under extreme foreign pressure. In view of this is it realistic to expect that citizens of other countries will be able to expect the Kremlin to adhere to principles of civilized conduct or to abide by written documents which do not serve its political and military interests? A question raised by Anthony Lewis in *The New York Times* of September 24, 1973 was never really answered. A portion of this column follows:

> . . . Before Leonid Brezhnev came to the United States last June, the Panovs were told that they would get their visas if they stilled all publicity about their cases during the summer, as they did. On August 9 that commitment was officially confirmed to an American visitor in Moscow, Robert Abrams, borough president of the Bronx, N. Y. A Soviet deputy interior minister named Viktorov, with other high officials present, told Abrams that Panov "will positively be able to leave."
>
> Last month the authorities again rejected the Panovs' visa applications. Two weeks ago Panov was told that he

might still be allowed to go—alone, if he abandoned [his wife]. He said no.

Henry Kissinger is fighting in Congress against any conditions on American trade concessions to the Soviet Union. In answer to questions at his confirmation hearings he suggested that the United States, rather than trying to "transform the domestic structure of societies with which we deal," should aim to affect "the foreign policy of those societies."

The Panov story indicates one major fallacy in that Kissinger proposition: It is not possible to divide a system like the Soviet Union's into neat "domestic" and "foreign" aspects. A powerful Government that breaks its word at home, that practices vindictive cruelty toward its own citizens without any moral or political constraints, can hardly be trusted abroad.

It is of course not only the arbitrary barriers to Jewish emigration that arouse concern about the U.S.S.R. The violent suppression of dissent, the fearful inhibitions on contacts with foreigners—these things are disturbing in foreign policy terms precisely because a society so isolated is not likely to be a rational and reliable partner in international life.

For those very reasons, opening the Soviet system to a freer flow of ideas and persons has been a major aim of Western policy for years. It is, for example, at the current European Security Conference. Those who feel strongly about pursuing that goal are not against détente; they only fear what Andrei Sakharov, the Soviet scientist, has rightly called "the danger of seeming détente, not accompanied by increasing trust or democratization. . . ."

The question stands unanswered; if a government cannot be trusted at home, how can it be trusted abroad? If the Russian people themselves can't trust the Kremlin, we need to talk about why anyone thinks Americans can.

It may also be reasonable to assume that if the U.S. had an internal system like that of the U.S.S.R., we would need "enemies" as much as they do and our dealings with other states would be much like the dealings of Russia. Conversely, to have a foreign policy as heedless and ruthless as Russia's, we would almost of necessity require an internal system as primitively repressive as that administered by the Kremlin. An informed and influential U.S. populace would never tolerate an arbitrary invasion of Canada or Mexico. Similarly, an informed and influential Soviet populace would never have tolerated the Soviet invasions of Hungary and Czechoslovakia.

The difficulties of emigrating from the Soviet Union are well known. Less publicized is the fact that moving from one place to another within Russia is not a right but a privilege that must be earned. While still living in Russia, Alexander Solzhenitsyn complained bitterly to Soviet authorities about not being allowed to live with his family in Moscow. If an "internal passport" system were instituted in the U.S., Americans would rightly accuse the Federal Government of intolerable repression. The full range of suppression of constitutional rights in the Soviet Union suggests that the relationship which exists between the Soviet Government and the Soviet people is not one of cooperation but one of domination. Free people, in a cooperative relationship with duly elected representatives, should not have to tolerate such outrages. The question persists. If the Kremlin doesn't cooperate with Soviet peoples but dominates them instead in a system of isolation and confinement, why does anyone think the Kremlin will cooperate with Americans, in establishing better relations that are in our best interest? Can internal and external policies of a government ever really be separated?

The news media are full of reports which point to the Soviet desire and need to maintain isolation, confinement, internal tensions and the ongoing ideological struggle with a wide array of "enemies" which have been deliberately selected and designated as such. When the Soviet Union is really ready for better relations with the rest of the world, the walls and wire will come down, the isolation and confinement will end, no more "enemies" will be needed and thought-control, the artificial conditioning to fear and hatred of other societies, will cease. It seems unlikely that the Kremlin will do all or any of these things. But to the interested observer it also seems unlikely that under the present conditions there can be any genuine better relations in the sense of any meaningful, enduring cooperation.

When the Kremlin is finally able to demonstrate that it cooperates with Soviet peoples in their best interests, we may accept its profession of interest in cooperative relationships with other countries including the U.S. Perhaps it is perfectly reasonable to expect the Kremlin to treat Americans more favorably than it treats Russians. But no one is saying how. And no one wants to start any discernible public discussion on the question.

Perhaps there is inaccessible information or seldom-repeated questions or forgotten considerations that could make it entirely clear how we can expect trade to change all the things that are reported and lead to better relations between the U.S. and Russia. Perhaps the reports which come to the attention of the layman are unfair, lopsided or misleading. Perhaps it could all be cleared up by review of the information which may have become lost in the shuffle. Perhaps it could all be clarified by public discussion so that we could calm our fears and relax in the confident assurance that trade will indeed bring better relations between the U.S. and U.S.S.R. But the intellectuals and leading thinkers we depend on for views and opinions are keeping very quiet. They are seeing to it that we will never know. They are seeing to it that there will be no discernible public discussion on any ongoing basis which could resemble an educational process.

Some people will insist that trade will make the Kremlin harder to deal with by making it more secure and better able to manage its own affairs and manipulate those not yet under direct control. Is trade going to "mellow" the Kremlin if it increases Soviet power? Will it lead to "better relations" with Russia if we help solve economic problems brought on by their heavy military spending in the Middle East, Africa and elsewhere? Some people seem to think we may be asking for more of the same kind of trouble that erupted in the Middle East in 1973. Is there any validity in these views?

If we would ask questions we might find some of the influential people are asking us to disregard some of the difficult lessons we have had the opportunity to learn. Did the 1972 grain deal lead to peaceful cooperation in the Middle East or Southeast Asia? There has been no ongoing discussion as to how this made the Kremlin less suspicious or more cooperative. There is no public discussion as to whether this lowered or even moved any of the barriers against better relations.

The U.S. taxpayer subsidized the grain deal, subsidized the loan rate and partly guaranteed the loan itself. The U.S. taxpayer paid higher prices for food, not just bread, for that grain deal. If that didn't lead to "better relations," what hope is there that other deals will? How much more obliging can we be?

None of the leading thinkers in foreign policy want to get together and publicly discuss the question of how we can have anything but temporary "better relations" or cooperation with a government which quite openly pursues a policy of domination at home and in neighboring countries, quite frankly states that cooperation with other kinds of societies (except as a tactic for advantage, such as trade) is contrary to concepts of class struggle and other elements of Communist theology. How or why do we think trade is going to change this? Dead silence.

There are several interesting corollaries to the doctrine that trade will lead to better relations between the U.S. and Russia. One of these is that we "owe" Russia not only trade but credits, as if by withholding either we are denying them something that is rightly theirs. A similar notion was expressed in an editorial in *The New York Times* of January 2, 1975:

(The pertinent text is in *italics* supplied by the author. *The New York Times* requires that when its editorials are reprinted, that they be reprinted in their entirety.)

41

The Soviet press campaign against the emigration clauses in the new Trade Reform Act suggests an intention to repudiate the three-way compromise on this issue negotiated by Secretary Kissinger with Moscow and Senate leaders. For the Soviet Union to do so would be as short-sighted as was the action of the Senate in arbitrarily attempting to limit Export-Import Bank credits to the insignificant sum of $300-million over four years.

The credit ceiling undoubtedly will have to be lifted if essential progress in expanding Soviet-American trade and joint development projects is to proceed as it should. Within limits set by economic feasibility, national security and mutual national interest, a substantial growth in commerce and investment should be possible. It is hard to see how a more normal relationship between the two superpowers can be achieved without it. The economic relationship is fundamental to the détente that everyone favors—or claims to favor.

It has been evident since 1971 that the underlying transaction in the new Soviet-American relationship has been a Soviet offer of détente to obtain Western technology and credits and an American offer of trade and credits to obtain détente. All the elements in the evolving Soviet-American relationship, as a result, have been linked together. Gains in nuclear arms control, the Berlin settlement, progress toward a settlement in the Middle East and peace in Indochina, as well as new hopes on human rights issues, such as Jewish emigration from the Soviet Union, have all stemmed from détente. They are, in fact, the definition of détente.

The nature of this transaction justifies pressure by Americans for more progress on all these fronts, but only on condition that arbitrary limits are not placed on the American side of the bargain. A strong Administration lead will be essential in the new Congress if such arbitrary limits on credits, investment and trade are to be lifted.

There are valid concerns that Soviet trade, carried on by the state, is calculated to serve national interests, while free American businessmen, essentially motivated by profits, are inadequately guided by governmental

42

authority to assure that national as well as private interests are served. Action to meet these concerns would strengthen an Administration move to loosen credit restrictions on East-West trade.

All this will take time. Meanwhile, the Trade Reform Act has authorized the removal of tariff and credit discrimination against the Soviet Union for 18 months. Annual Presidential extensions afterward clearly will depend not only on the freer emigration policies that the act requires, but on the whole context of détente.

Whether Soviet "assurances" or only "elucidations" of policy on emigration were given is a matter of semantics. Secretary Kissinger clearly had reason to believe, on the basis of many discussions with Soviet leaders, that freer emigration would occur. It would be a serious error for Moscow to disappoint these expectations. But the error would be as great on the American side if the Congress, by maintaining credit restrictions, weakened the Administration's negotiating hand not only on emigration but across the whole range of détente-related issues that will determine the prospects for peace.

The thrust of this argument is that nothing in relations between the U.S. and Russia can succeed unless we offer trade and credits, with the credits presumably at preferential rates not available to American taxpayers who might like to buy a home or an automobile. As long as we agree to offer trade and credits, the argument goes, things will go forward, there will be détente.

There never was any real public discussion by leading thinkers in foreign policy as to why the Soviet Union needs subsidized credits or any credits at all. Russia has a gross national product second only to ours. Russia is an exporter of oil and other minerals; it is rich in natural resources. Any time Russia really needs money, all it has to do is divert some of its resources from the production of conventional weapons such as submarines or tanks.

If there were discussion of the question among influential people, we might find there is no obvious reason to treat

43

the Soviet Union as an underdeveloped country. No one wants to raise the question of whether we are doing this and if so why, or raise questions which represent other possible viewpoints. It is as if everyone is afraid they might not like the outcome, that their argument or view may appear to be a casualty.

If Russia is an underdeveloped country in terms of goods and services available to the populace, there are many reported facts which could lead one to believe that Russia isn't underdeveloped militarily. If there were discussion, we might even find that it is not really the fault of the West in general that Russia refuses to divert more spending to the civilian sector of the economy.

The Soviet Union has consistently refused to agree to treaties on weapons testing and disarmament because of its objections to inspection and verification requirements acceptable to other countries. It is likely that Russia has brought economic troubles not only on itself but on other countries trying to keep pace with its weapons production, especially the means to oppose Soviet conventional weapons such as submarines and river-fording tanks.

A discussion among influential people might indeed indicate that we "owe" Russia subsidized credits, that this view is most easily reconciled with reported facts. Or discussion might indicate that there is little reason to assume that we "owe" Russia subsidized credits. But representatives of both views seem to be deathly afraid of putting their doctrines on the line in public discussion. Their intellectual "do not disturb" signs are too obvious.

Another assumption often found lurking in statements, columns and editorials such as the one cited above is more ominous. There is a dark hint that we give Russia trade and credits or there will be hell to pay—trade and credits or else!

It is easy for the casual observer to get the impression that many influential people think it is up to the U.S. to offer trade and credits to get détente, either in the sense of "cooperation" or "coexistence." The implication is that we had better buy them off. It is quite true that we will probably get

44

paid for what we send them but the advanced computers they are getting could be of incalculable value to them in drawing away from the West in the arms race. For the "going price" of such items they permanently acquire priceless advanced technology that can give them economic, industrial and military advantages, any or all of which could in the long run be decisive. No one knows what sort of showdown the Soviets may choose against those who oppose them, or where or when.

The implication in many statements is that as long as we keep giving them irretrievable technology in exchange for tentative détente, for some sort of elusive "good will" which can be turned on and off like an electric light, things will be pleasant. But if we stop helping them engineer their economic, industrial and military ascendancy over the West, there will be trouble.

There are many statements implying that if we don't give Russia trade and credits, the Kremlin will begin to stir up all the trouble it could stir up in all the trouble spots around the world, that détente is what keeps the lid on. If we give the Soviet Communists what they want, they will go easy on us, at least for the time being. Never mind all those tanks and submarines they are building for an eventual confrontation with somebody, somewhere, sometime.

If we are trying to "buy off" an aggressive power, it should be observed that history throws an inauspicious light on such attempts.

From the opinions of the influential people it could be easy to get the impression that what we are getting out of détente is a sort of ongoing reprieve from things Russia might do if there were no détente. But the influential people, the leading thinkers in foreign policy are absolutely determined not to have any public discussion of the question of whether we are pursuing our détente policies under a threat of a return to the "cold war days." It may well be possible to demonstrate that there is no threat involved. But it looks as if we will never know. But if we are acting in response to a threat, this is more properly called blackmail than détente.

45

Advocates of trade and credits for Russia often talk about trade as a means of "talking with those people and breaking the ice" or as a means of "communicating with the Russians" in order to "build good will." But according to reports available to the general public, the trouble is that we are dealing with those who represent only 5% of the Russian people, who are members of the Party, who are furthering their own interests at the expense of their countrymen, who are consolidating and extending their own power and who intend to see to it that there isn't much good will between ordinary Russians and Americans.

From available information it appears that in dealing with the Soviet Communist Party members we are dealing with those who have willingly and freely chosen to enter into a servant-master relationship with their own countrymen, with themselves as masters. Many who have done so have been quoted as mentioning "a better career" and "travel abroad" as self-serving motives for seeking Party membership.

Reports available to the general public indicate that this 5% of the Soviet people represent no one but themselves. They use the human and natural resuorces of a vast continent as their private property to pursue their narrow interests which are in conflict with the broad interests of the Russian and Soviet peoples and the peoples of most of the rest of the world. This 5% ruling elite is perfectly willing to risk nuclear war, if that is necessary, to maintain their power through thought-control and minority rule, the confinement and isolation of their populations and the populations of the Soviet bloc. Control is maintained basically by fear—the Soviet and satellite peoples are constantly reminded of the "fact" that the outside world is hostile to them and awaiting any chance to take advantage of them.

The 5% ruling elite is perfectly willing to promote limited peripheral armed conflicts, hoping these conflicts don't get out of hand and lead to nuclear war. But if they do, it is just too bad and it is a calculated gamble they are willing to accept in order to maintain themselves in power.

What often seems to be forgotten is that this 5% ruling

elite in Russia appears to be willing to do anything, or risk anything, regardless of the consequences for all of mankind, including themsleves, in order to cling to power. At times U.S. Government officials don't seem to keep this in mind. Our officials seem to think, for example, that what is unthinkable to us is also unthinkable to Soviet leaders. However, this seems to be at least questionable. It is reported that the Soviet Union has plans to hold its casualties to about ten million in the event of a nuclear exchange. It was reported recently that the United States had plans, or lack of plans, to sustain casualties of about 90 million people.

From time to time information will appear which gives insight into the minds of the Soviet ruling elite. The *New York Times* of October 22, 1975 printed a translated article by the Soviet dissident historian and writer Andrei Amalrik. The following were some of the pertinent passages:

> ... Whether or not the American leaders recognize it, a fundamental change in the foreign policy of the U.S.S.R. is impossible without a change in its internal situation.
>
> It is difficult to imagine a state combining constant suppression and violence internally with peaceful behavior and accommodation externally. Such "peaceful behavior" could only be the consequence of military weakness or of deceptive camouflage. . . .
>
> . . . The mentality of government officials (in the Soviet Union) rising to foreign policy leadership has been shaped for years by dealing with internal political problems, and all the methods they have mastered inside the country are applied abroad.
>
> American domestic policies are based on a play of free forces, settled by compromise, while Soviet domestic policies are based on a no-compromise implementation of instructions. And while the U.S. may sit down at the negotiating table consciously or subconsciously thinking of compromise, the U.S.S.R. sits down with intention of achieving its objectives in full, agreeing only to fictitious concessions.
>
> The other strange feature of American policy, as with

the policy of the West in general, is the treatment of the U.S.S.R. like a small child who must be allowed everything and not be irritated because he might start screaming—all because, they say, when it grows up it will understand everything.

This prolonged "upbringing" of the U.S.S.R. by the methods of Dr. Spock is reflected not only in an endless number of minor concessions by the U.S. but also actions that are simply humiliating for its prestige as a big power. This was most clearly illustrated by the reluctance of President Ford to invite Aleksandr I. Solzhenitsyn to the White House because Mr. Kissinger feared this would infuriate Leonid I. Brezhnev. . . .

Knowing the character of those whom the Americans are trying to play up to by such behavior, I believe that even though it wins approval from their side it also arouses a degree of contempt. . . .

This raises the obvious, awkward question of what good it does to try to "get on the good side" of such people. What chance is there to attempt to establish "good will" in dealing with this ruling elite? There has been an absolute minimum of public discussion of how we can hope to "communicate with the Russians" when we so rarely have the opportunity, in commercial enterprises, to talk with anyone who represents the other 95% of the Russian people and can convey our good wishes and good will.

There may be simple answers to the questions raised here. There may be other questions that cancel them out. But apparently the advocates and opponents of the idea of trade as "opening communications" each lack confidence in their views. Each appears unwilling to challenge the other to put his ideas alongside reported facts and attempt to reconcile the two.

It may seem as if the information cited here as a potential challenge to slogans is common knowledge. Why repeat what everybody knows? The suggestion that this information be brought into play in discussion is based on the assumption that it is not a question of what we know but a question of what knowledge we use in forming our guiding assumptions. If we have knowledge, it does not necessarily follow from this that we will take the knowledge into account.

The intent here is not to provide new information or to recite old information but to ask whether information has a proper influence on our thought, on our determination of guiding assumptions.

The inherent danger of slogans which represent substitutes for thinking is that they have the power to make us forget, disregard, minimize or suppress pertinent knowledge. If we insulate our slogans against reported facts, through laziness or wishful thinking, we might as well live under a system in which information is officially suppressed because, in effect, it is voluntarily suppressed. This is less vicious than official suppression but it still has adverse potential consequences.

If nobody mentions what everybody knows, if we all proceed to disseminate slogans which can't be reconciled with reported facts, there isn't much point in having freedom of information and freedom to discuss the information. We have access to reported facts but are these reported facts reflected in our ideas, slogans and guiding assumptions regarding domestic and foreign policy?

Using knowledge we have in order to test ideas and slogans may be something that can't happen in newspaper stories or in syndicated columns. Perhaps such testing can only happen in discussion. A columnist who wants to advance a certain view will hardly introduce reported facts which would bring the view into question. It may take two people to make full use of knowledge, to make sure it is used to test ideas and slogans.

A reported fact in a clipping in a drawer isn't going to be used to test ideas. However, a reported fact in the form of a question, presented in a fashion in which it can't be ignored, is going to be taken into account whether anyone one likes it or not. The person questioned is going to have to discredit it or act and speak as if aware of it.

It is not only a question of what we know but what we use to match against what is said. It is a question of whether pertinent reported facts can resist slogans, the wishful thinking, the minimizing, all the devices used to get rid of them when they interfere with what certain influential people want to believe. It may, finally, be a question of whether facts can survive not only official censorship but voluntary suppression.

It could be said that if columnists, for example, had to take all reported facts into account, this burden would deprive them of some of their more abrasive views, lessen their effectiveness as agitators and advocates of unpopular opinions, which certainly are necessary in the system we have. It is quite possible that being expected or required to take all reported facts into account, not only those "friendly" to a certain viewpoint, would be a burden for some. But there are several questions.

Is it an unfair or unreasonable burden? If an opinion or viewpoint rests on the omission of certain pertinent reported facts, if it is dependent on the reader having forgotten or not having awareness of certain items of news, is the point worth making? Should a columnist ask us or require us to suspend knowledge or judgment or both in order to accept his thesis? Is it presumptuous, at least, for a responsible influential person to do this?

The issue here is not whether trade will lead to détente or what détente means. The issue is whether we should accept or reject the idea that trade will lead to détente without public discussion.

If détente is in our interest and if trade will lead to more or better détente, we shouldn't take action that will lead to a return to the cold war. If détente is a "one way street" as some have charged, we shouldn't pursue it to a unilateral Soviet advantage. The issue here is whether there has been enough public discussion to give the American people a basis for judging what we are doing now and what we ought to be doing if it turns out we ought to be doing something different.

It is doubtful there can ever be agreement as to what we are doing and what we ought to be doing. But discussion could produce a consensus where more people favor one view

over various other views. It could be a basis for a better understanding of what problems confront us and what solutions
are available. But the influential people show no inclination
to engage in such discussion for the benefit of themselves or
of the public, in an effort to see what can be explained and
what can't.

4

International Meddling

"We are meddling in the internal affairs of Russia if we ask them for concessions on civil rights" is an idea often repeated by some influential people.

In an ideal world, no nation would meddle in the internal affairs of any other nation. In an ideal world, each nation could entrust its independence and security to the good will of every other nation. In such a world there would never be any need or any reason for any nation to meddle in the affairs of any other nation. But unfortunately there seems little prospect that we will soon be living in such a world.

As a matter of principle it is probably true that the U.S. shouldn't meddle in the internal affairs of the Soviet Union. But it is also true, as a matter of principle, that Russia shouldn't meddle in the internal affairs of other countries. If there is some vague international understanding or diplomatic courtesy which forbids meddling in the internal affairs of other countries, it appears to have been violated by the Soviet Union.

It isn't necessary to be a diplomat or a State Department official to be aware of Soviet meddling. Readily accessible news media often furnish information on this topic. For example, the September 29, 1974 *New York Times* carried the following column by Robert Conquest:

> Recent revelations about the Central Intelligence Agency's activities in Chile and elsewhere raise the question of the nature and extent of comparable actions by its great rival, the K.G.B., the Soviets' Committee of

Government Security. In fact there is a good deal of knowledge available, not from the Soviet press or Government, but from victims or intended victims who found out the hard way.

The K.G.B. is not simply a mirror-image of the C.I.A. (or even the C.I.A. plus the Federal Bureau of Investigation). One difference was demonstrated a couple of weeks ago when *Pravda* announced the award, on his 70th birthday, of the Order of the October revolution to Semyon Ignatiev who was Stalin's last head of the organization and who was responsible for, among other things, the notorious doctor's plot purge. Yuri Andropov, the current K.G.B. chief, got the Order of Lenin and the title Hero of Socialist Labor earlier, after a speech in which President Nicolai Podgorny praised his "strengthening and improving this important sector of state activity."

The sort of fears about the C.I.A. that have arisen in the United States have no parallel in Soviet concerns about the K.G.B.

The C.I.A. and the K.G.B. also differ in size and resources. Perhaps 6 of every 10 Soviet diplomats and other representatives abroad are K.G.B. personnel; those not directly employed must also help out when called upon.

In 1971, the British expelled 105 members of the Soviet Embassy staff. Espionage figured largely in the British Government's explanation for its action, but it was also established that British intelligence had discovered plans for sabotage, not only of military installations but also of such things as water supplies.

The British incident was by no means a lone example. Since 1960, at least 380 Soviet diplomats have been expelled from their posts in 40 countries on all six continents. Oddly enough, men expelled by one country frequently turn up—without even a name change—in neighboring capitals.

Not that operations are always conducted through embassies. Sometimes the route is more direct. That was the case with arms supplied to the Provisional faction of the Irish Republican Army, several tons of which, en route from Prague to the Ulster terrorists, were seized at Amsterdam in October, 1971.

Financial intervention to support pro-Soviet elements is old-established practice but does not necessarily go through K.G.B. channels, since practically every other Soviet channel is secret too. Communist parties have long been so funded; the details of subventions to the Italian Communist party, again via Prague, were established 20 years ago. Recently there have been other examples including the discovery by Mexican officials in 1968, and by Brazilians in 1972, of scores of thousands of dollars concealed in the luggage of party officials returning from Moscow. The Colombians, in 1968, intercepted a $100,000 subsidy to terrorists, by the K.G.B. itself.

And when it comes to such matters as coups and plots, the last three years alone have seen the organization of the Ali Sabry plot against the regime in Egypt (1971); the plot against Gen. Gaafer al-Nimiery in the Sudan (1971); the organization, arming and training of guerrillas, for which five Soviet diplomats were expelled from Mexico (1971); a plot in Rumania (1972); plots in Bolivia and Colombia for which Soviet diplomats and others were expelled (1972); a plot in Tunisia with the same results (1973); the recently discovered plot in Yugoslavia. There, on September 12, Marshall Tito referred publicly to a case that had been brewing for some months and which involved the arrest and forthcoming trial of an underground "Stalinist" grouping, which relied on help from "abroad" and whose leaders are old Soviet nominees and K.G.B. contacts.

The fact that some of these occurred in Communist countries was no phenomenon. Earlier examples included the Soviet-sponsored "Natolin" plot against Wladyslaw Gomulka in 1956, and Admiral Teme Sejko's conspiracy in Albania in 1964. They even extended to Cuba where, in 1968, several Soviet diplomats and others were denounced and expelled for organizing and supporting an attempt to seize power.

Later, of course, differences between Premier Fidel Castro and Moscow were largely accommodated, and the

Cuban secret service has been largely financed by Moscow for operations in South America, just as the Czechoslovak equivalent is the K.G.B.'s favored auxiliary in Western Europe. In the case of Chile, where the C.I.A.'s conduct is now under attack, it was through their Cuban subordinates that the K.G.B. directed the training of guerrillas. Their own direct operations in Chile were largely of the cash-and-organization type. In that, at least, there apparently is a parallel with the C.I.A.

While some of these reports may have been exaggerated by outraged officials in some of the offended countries, it seems questionable whether we can say that the Soviet Union scrupulously refrains from meddling in the internal affairs of other countries. If it is not correct to say this, it raises the awkward question of whether, by meddling in the internal affairs of other countries, the Soviet Union has forfeited its right to insist that other countries refrain from meddling in its affairs. If the Soviet Government meddles, why shouldn't other governments feel free to meddle back? International meddling seems to be such a sufficiently time-honored practice that a particular example shouldn't provoke extraordinary outrage.

Then there is the specific question as to whether the U.S. was meddling in the internal affairs of Russia by asking for concessions on civil rights in exchange for trade and credits. Probably so but it was also probably accurate to say it was a mild form of meddling in support of the Internation Declaration on Human Rights. Although it is true that Russia signed this Declaration and the United States did not, it may be preferable to live in a country that did not sign and allows its people to emigrate than in a country that signed the Declaration and imposes confinement and isolation backed by walls, wire, gun towers and minefields. The government which upholds the principles may have as much right to support them as the government which signed the document.

If there were any serious public discussion by leading thinkers of the question of whether we are meddling in the internal affairs of the Soviet Union, it might be determined or agreed on that it is quite true but that it is only half the truth. If the matter were discussed, questions and answers might indicate that while we were meddling in Russia's internal affairs, there is another side to it that is not repeated as often. There is no way of knowing what the discussion might bring out but it is possible that in view of the meddling Russia does, our meddling is not really as outrageous and unjustified as popular doctrine and slogan might indicate.

The question has rightly been asked, here and abroad, "How would we like it if Russia publicly demanded greater civil rights reform in the U.S. before trading with us?" If there were informed public discussion by experts on foreign relations there might be agreement that Soviet insistence on more school busing or more equal opportunity would not really be the equivalent of U.S. insistence on the right of emigration from Russia. Or discussion might show that the comparison is valid indeed. But the influential people are seeing to it that the general public will never have the necessary public discussion on which to base an informed and reasoned conclusion.

If there were discussion, hypothetical situations might be advanced which in effect "turn the tables" for clearer perspective.

For example, if the U.S. Government cut us off from the rest of the world, imposed thought-control, instilled fear and hatred of other social systems, kept us in a constant state of psychological readiness for any sort of conflict with Russia, jammed foreign broadcasts, invaded Canada and Mexico and a few other countries, held their populations captive behind barbed wire and minefields and then announced its intention to dominate the world, wouldn't we expect Russians to meddle in our internal affairs? If we were building three times as many submarines and five times as many tanks as Russians, wouldn't they be justified in wondering what we intended to do with them? Wouldn't they be foolish not to try to protect their interests? Wouldn't they use all available "dirty tricks" to attempt to short-circuit the uncontrollable bureaucratic

56

Frankenstein in Washington? Wouldn't they justify intervention by saying we had forfeited our right to immunity from meddling? If Soviet violations of human rights were limited to such things as lack of school busing, hardly anyone would say our violations of human rights and other transgressions were comparable to theirs.

The public discussion which is missing from our experience, and from our resources which we use to attempt to maintain our system, might examine the question of whether it is really accurate to say that the confinement and isolation of Soviet peoples and the peoples of neighboring countries is the equivalent of such things as the lack of school busing in the U.S. or the failure to prosecute those responsible for the Kent State Massacre. It may be quite a valid comparison or it may be comparing "apples and oranges" or there may be other comparisons which would be more valid.

To an observer lacking in expertise the facts may seem overly simple. It appears that violations of human rights are unconstitutional in Russia and in the United States. In the United States, with admitted zig-zags and setbacks, we are attempting to enforce our laws. The information available makes it appear that the courts in the Soviet Union are making no comparable effort. There is no doubt that in the United States, rights of minorities are violated by the majority. But in the U.S.S.R., it seems to be the other way round. With the connivance of the courts, a 5% minority violates the rights of the 95% majority by exercising absolute, unquestioned, unchallenged power over them, except when foreign governments and organizations can intervene, as in the case of Valery Panov and his wife. This seems to be a big difference. Perhaps discussion might indicate that it is only a small difference. But we have little prospect of finding out.

On the surface it would appear that the U.S. efforts on behalf of Soviet minorities and by extension all Soviet peoples is not as rude and not as violent as the Soviet invasions of Hungary and Czechoslovakia. There is argument about "spheres of influence" but Hungary is not Russia. Czechoslovakia is not Russia. The U.S. effort on behalf of would-be

57

emigrants from Russia may be more direct and open than Soviet activities or the activities of Moscow-oriented Communists in France, Italy or Portugal. The use of an alien-influenced political party seems to be a "one-way street" since one looks in vain for a Liberal or Labor or Democratic Party in Russia. No one wants to talk about what seems to be an obvious question. If Russia insists on the right (in Soviet theology it is the duty) to interfere in the internal affairs of other countries, and insists on non-interference in its own affairs, isn't this clearly a double standard? Why should anyone feel obliged to accept such a double standard?

A corollary to the "meddling" doctrine is that we are "imposing our idea of morality" on the Russians by asking for more civil rights in Russia. If there were public discussion, it might be brought out that civil rights wasn't our idea. Freedom to travel, emigrate and read foreign publications are not really the exclusive property of Americans. If there were discussion there might even be consensus that the desire for these rights is common to humanity. Don't Russians have as much curiosity and wanderlust as anyone else? Are we assuming some people don't want the right to information, the right to travel, the right to emigrate? Who, for example?

If there were public discussion we might be able to acknowledge the human right not to be confined and isolated and subject to thought-control and minority rule. We might be able to agree that strict controls in Russia prove that the Russian people have the same desire for rights that other people have. We might be able to agree that, if we assume that the Russian people have some separate endowment of intelligence, curiosity or moral principle which enables them to enjoy and take pride in the restrictions imposed on them, we presume their inferiority as a people or a race. Or there may not be any agreement on these questions or the consensus may go the other way. But at least we would have some basis for judgment.

It may seem to some people that these questions have been raised before and that they should have been settled. Should we still be hearing slogans about "sovereign" governments which no one has a right to question? Some people might feel justified in saying that finally, at some point, we have to get over the idea that governments are sacred, that governments have divine right, that governments are laws unto themselves and no one may interfere, that governments have a right to do whatever they have the power to do. These ideas did so much damage to the world in the 1930's and 1940's it would seem profitable to review a bit of history.

If we say it is wrong to try to influence Kremlin policies of repression, aren't we saying a government has a right to do whatever it has the power to do? Isn't this saying, in effect, might makes right? Do we really mean to say this?

Some people have a tendency to accept what is going on in the Soviet Union as "normal" for the Soviet peoples. For example, Senator Claiborne Pell, Democrat of Rhode Island, wrote in the August 9, 1974 issue of *The New York Times* as follows:

> . . . I am under no illusions as to any sun and light behind the Iron Curtain.
> But at least people there are alive and leading reasonably normal lives. It is not the bleak scorched area it could be in a World War III. . . .

This may leave a reader wondering what is "normal" about being almost totally cut off from civilization under a system of thought-control and minority rule in a state of isolation and confinement. One wonders whether Senator Pell would consider it normal or even tolerable for him to live in a system where those who are allowed to leave their homeland are often considered the lucky ones. If there were discussion, we might find that to say that such a life in the Soviet Union is "normal" or even "reasonably normal" is to impose a double standard which presumes the moral or intellectual inferiority of the Soviet peoples. There are others who will insist there should be a double standard, that "those people over there in Russia have been living under tyranny for cen-

59

turies," as if they ought to be used to it by now, or as if they would get used to it if they had any sense.

There are many other questions which suggest themselves and which could be discussed if the influential people were inclined to do so. It is assumed by many, for example, that what is going on in Russia is only an "internal affair." But does this assumption really warrant being treated as a self-evident truth?

An internal doctrine which requires social systems to be "enemies" instead of friends almost invariably kills or cripples cooperation between that society and other kinds of societies. Such an internal doctrine requires massive military spending not only by the society that designates others as "enemies" but by the "enemies" themselves. Virtually all the world's problems which are the most urgent would require cooperation among peoples, societies and governments if the problems were to be solved. If the solutions which can be achieved by cooperation are in effect "vetoed" by those who insist on artificial tension and conflict as a means of preserving their status as a ruling elite, as a means of maintaining themselves in power, by those who have learned to profit from the "enemies" system, is this an internal affair or something which affects everyone in the world? These are only a few of the loose ends which are lying about waiting for public discussion.

The questions raised here are not intended to imply that the U.S. should subvert, undermine or overthrow the Soviet system. The questions are intended merely to ask why we need to respect the sovereignty of a government which doesn't respect the sovereignty of any other government. There may be perfectly satisfactory answers to the questions or solutions to the issues raised. But there has been no significant public discussion of these matters which would enable the interested observer to reconcile what some people are saying with what is reported in the news media. The influential people have left the laymen to shift for themselves.

The issue here is not whether we are meddling in the internal affairs of Russia or whether we should meddle. The

60

issue here is whether opinions and slogans will be tossed about as if they were facts, whether we will have public discussion on what we are doing and whether we should be doing it. The issue is whether we will accept judgments without questions and answers.

If we are interfering in the internal affairs of Russia and this is unwarranted, we certainly should stop. If a certain amount of meddling in the affairs of Russia or other countries is necessary to protect our interests, we should certainly protect our interests. The influential people, by their strict adherence to The Rules against public discussion, are not providing the general public with a basis for judgment. All we get are conflicting opinions from equally respected politicians, professors, experts, officials and journalists who are presumably responding to the same set of reported facts. They seem to have made up their minds and don't want to risk having their opinions disturbed by direct questions about what everybody knows.

Pertinent reported facts are readily available. It is not a question of whether we have knowledge but whether we will think and act as if we are aware of the reported facts.

5

Blame for International Tensions

"The U.S. is principally to blame, or as much to blame as Russia for the cold war and world tensions." It has long been fashionable to speak of Russia and the United States as "two superpowers" competing for "spheres of influence." They are often lumped together in terms which imply they are equally wicked in motive and evil in design, without any qualification or distinction as to overall aims or intents. Many professors, politicians, experts, officials and journalists speak and write as if they believe that any nation which has allowed itself to become a superpower and allowed itself to become involved in opposing the aims of the Soviet bloc must be equally to blame with Russia. If the U.S. sends arms to foreign countries to be used to counter forces using Soviet arms, according to statements of some influential people, U.S. motives in doing so must be exactly the same as those of the U.S.S.R.

It would seem to be axiomatic in international relations that a great power carries with it the responsibility to use this power judiciously and not in a way which causes disruption and tensions in international life. For reasons which are never discussed in public by influential people, the U.S. has been held to stricter standards of conduct because better behavior is "expected" of a system with a representative form of government often referred to as "democracy." If the Soviet Union indulges in violence, duplicity and disruption, well, that is "expected" because they have a different "system." There doesn't seem to be any objective reason why Russia shouldn't act with a measure of responsibility and restraint commensurate with its power and influence, regardless of what "system" they have. It is what circumstances require. But there is an expectation conditioning which has gradually grown up and insinuated itself into our thinking and which is, of course, never discussed in public by influential people.

By now perhaps it is less a question of who may have started international tensions or the cold war (or, if cold war is considered an offensive term, the "current détente") than a question of who is perpetuating the tensions today. Due to the indications that a double standard has sprung up—what is permitted for the Soviet is taboo for the U.S.—it might be well to ask how other countries would react if the U.S. did some of the things the Soviet does.

If the U.S. Government imposed on Americans the isolation and confinement the Soviet imposes on its peoples, Western Europeans would be apoplectic. Latin American nations would break diplomatic relations and the "non-aligned" nations (after consultation with Russia) would demand that the U.S. be censured in the United Nations. But the U.N. committee allegedly responsible for human rights would ignore any gulag archipelago that existed in the U.S., as it ignores the one in Russia, and would continue its custom of taking refuge in safer investigations such as the problem of forced marriages in Tanzania.

Then let us suppose the United States Government instituted other practices which have been followed in the Soviet Union for years.

If the U.S. Government officially denounced "a general human approach" as Soviet officials reportedly have done, in favor of class struggle, pitting capitalism against all other systems and declaring that capitalism must be victorious, there would be outraged howls of protest against a barbaric ideology contributing to international tensions. If the U.S. Government took over radio or television transmitters and ordered many of them to broadcast nothing but meaningless noise in order to keep us from hearing Canadian broadcasts, this would certainly be condemned. If the U.S. acquired satellite countries and surrounded them with impenetrable physical barriers, this would surely be denounced as an aggressive action endangering world peace. In other words, the U.S. would be universally condemned for doing what the Soviet Union has been doing for years. This must tell us something about which country is primarily responsible for world tensions. But the double standard also tells something about the expectation conditioning which has quietly crept into our way of looking at ourselves and others.

There are doubtless many cases in which the U.S. failed to make agreements that it might successfully have concluded with the Soviet Union. The U.S. undoubtedly has made many mistakes in dealing with Russia and with other countries. The U.S. undoubtedly overreacted to some perceived threats, thus temporarily disturbing security and confidence among nations. But it often appears that the U.S. is blamed more for its excesses and errors than the Soviet Union is blamed for deliberate policies of isolation and confinement of its own people and for the disruption and tension which results from its frankly admitted efforts to press for extension and consolidation of socialism and actions on behalf of "oppressed peoples" seeking "self-determination." The Soviet Union is "expected" to grasp for power at any opportunity; the U.S. is not even "expected" to make mistakes in attempting to counter such efforts.

The United States and Russia are often blamed equally for the perpetuation of the arms race. What is rarely discussed publicly by influential people is the fact that if the U.S. Government refused to accept inspection requirements which were acceptable to other powers in a proposed disarmament or troop reduction treaty, the U.S. citizen has a very good chance of finding out about it and doing something about it. The American people, for example, reportedly played a big role in the decision to stop the fighting in Indochina by cutting off U.S. arms and aid shipments to that area. Their opinion poll preferences and their letters and voices were heeded by their elected representatives. Unfortunately, the Russian people were in no position to exercise similar restraint on the flow of Russian arms to Indochina. Similarly, if the Soviet Union refuses to accept disarmament, troop reduction or limits on weapons testing on grounds that on-site inspection is an intrusion, the Soviet people have a very limited chance of finding out about it (hardly any Kremlin Papers are ever "leaked" to *Pravda*) let alone doing anything about it. The decades-long, duly recorded Soviet objection to treaty enforcement makes no difference. In the accepted, fashionable parlance, both side are equally to blame for the arms race and world tensions.

There seem to be many reported facts which at least on the surface seem difficult to reconcile with the idea that Russia and the U.S. are equally to blame for the remaining world tensions. If there were public discussion of the simple, obvious questions raised by these reported facts, there might not be agreement but we might have a better idea of whether statements and reports are compatible. But the professors, politicians, experts and officials continue to give the public their famous silent treatment.

How many Soviet newspapers are free of government control and how many U.S. publications are censored by the U.S. Government? Answers to these questions might help give us a basis for deciding who is to blame for tensions. Can government manipulation of communications media serve any constructive purpose, a purpose which is in the interest of the general public, mankind, civilization? Can such manipulation serve any purpose other than perpetuating thought-control and minority rule? The answers to these questions ought to say something about which government, the U.S. or Soviet, manipulates thought and emotion to perpetuate hostilities and tensions, to maintain the characteristic "enemies" relationship between peoples, the only atmosphere in which minority rule can prosper.

These questions, admittedly, deal with well-known facts. But it is not a question of whether we are aware of reported facts but whether we show it, whether we think and act as if we are aware of reported facts.

What is the purpose of the isolation and confinement, the

65

manipulation of whole continents full of people, if not to arrange it so a government has a virtually free hand in domestic and foreign affairs, so a government is answerable to no one except a small ruling elite, so a government can represent no one but itself? These questions are not based on obscure facts. The reported facts are available to anyone who reads news publications.

Wouldn't it be difficult for the Soviet Union to maintain its authority if there were no cold war tensions, no "enemies" to warn their people against and then reassure them of Soviet protection if they cooperate? Doesn't the Kremlin need the artificial hostility and isolation which are possible only through thought-control and minority rule?

Wouldn't it reduce tensions if there were no isolation and confinement of the people of Russia and China, if they had free access to all information from outside and were not taught to hate and fear foreigners, if they were permitted to travel freely to any country to see for themselves the ideas and conditions which prevail, whether other countries and peoples really are their "enemies"?

If it were not for thought-control and minority rule, the isolation and confinement of Soviet and Chinese peoples, the doctrines of class struggle, isn't it possible there might not be any cold war or international tensions?

If these people had the freedom of movement, the free access to information and the means to legally and peacefully remove individuals and political parties from power, as in the U.S., how could there be what we know as cold war tensions? Does anyone think the non-Communist Party Russian people, so generous and tolerant in spite of propaganda, would stand for the needless barriers and suspicions, for the total disregard of the Soviet Constitution that leads to purely artificial conflicts and to "enemies" relationships with other people, if they were aware of what was happening and could stop it?

Can we really say that a government which cuts itself and its people off from the rest of civilization is no more to blame for tensions than a government which permits free movement of people and ideas?

Wouldn't it be more accurate to say that those powers which have a vested interest in the isolation and confinement of their people, those powers which need thought-control and minority rule to remain in power, are responsible for the artificial divisions and hostilities that many still refer to as cold war tensions? Which form of government has the most to gain from international tensions? Which is totally dependent on international tensions for its survival and power?

Many people in the West have been conditioned to "expect" Russia and China to do things which perpetuate the cold war and international tensions. This expectation conditioning influences people to ignore or minimize divisive and disruptive tactics and their effects merely because they are considered inevitable, so why bother? For this reason, perhaps these tactics are rarely considered to be a source from which tensions originate without some provocation. Attention is more often shifted to the actions of nations which are not "expected" to act in similar fashion, to use force or coercion, even when it may be necessary to protect their interests. If certain questions are raised, Russia or China may be considered as sources of tensions. But if no questions are raised, chances are the U.S. will get the blame.

The difficulties of attempting to pry open a system of confinement and isolation can be seen in the Soviet objections to provisions of the 1975 European security agreement. What is considered "free movement of people and ideas" by Western countries is termed "interfering in our internal affairs" by the Soviet Government. Some influential people in the West who favor the notion of "free movement . . ." nevertheless express sympathy with the Soviet view that its sovereignty is being violated, as if they could have it both ways. In a credit to their frankness, Soviet officials are reported to have acknowledged that to permit an influx of Western ideas might lead to the "ideological disarmament" of the Soviet Union.

The "sovereignty" issue, so often raised by Soviet officials and those in the West who oppose attaching conditions to trade and credits for the Soviet Union, appears to be basically a defense against any attempt to let some air into a closed system. Too much understanding and good will could result in a wavering of discipline and "vigilance." A wavering of suspicion plus an intrusion of a "general human approach" or cooperation to solve the problems confronting the race of man could result in a threat to the absolute power of the Supreme Soviet. History offers few examples of rulers voluntarily relaxing their hold on absolute power. But there are those in the West and in other countries who will not consider the possibility that such a defensively closed system could be more responsible for the remaining cold war tensions than open systems such as the United States' social and political structure.

Discussion of the many obvious questions might indicate that the U.S. is indeed solely to blame, or more to blame than other powers, for the remains of the cold war and for international tensions. But at least it would be discussed. At least we wouldn't have the obstinate silence on the matter which we now have. If the influential people would discuss the matter on television, the public would have some better basis for judgment than the popular slogans which have gained the respectability of facts or truths, apparently, because no one questions them.

It has been said, for example, that the Voice of America, Radio Free Europe and other transmitting facilities aimed at the other 95% of Soviet and Soviet satellite listeners are "remnants of the cold war" as if the cold war and world tensions would end if only we would stop this needless nagging on the airwaves. It is easy to get from there to the impression that we and the Soviets are equally to blame for the cold war.

But there are other "remnants of the cold war" which tend to escape mention. One of these is the Berlin Wall. Another is the ugly, degrading, primitive barrier of barbed wire, gun towers and minefields reaching from the Soviet border with Norway to the Soviet border with Iran, except for inaccessible or unpopulated areas, and physically restraining either the Soviet peoples themselves or the populations of the Soviet satellites. Another relic of the past is the steady flow of anti-West propaganda, both inside and outside the Soviet Union,

68

proclaiming and extolling the suffocating philosophy that people of diverse "systems" must be "enemies," that there is to be no confidence, no cooperation, no hope for the prospect of a better world which could be possible in the absence of artificial fear and conflict. Another prominent antique is the mere fact of the isolation and confinement of Soviet and satellite peoples at a time when there is greater need than ever to be aware of and to take part in what is going on in the rest of the world, to be free to cooperate in dealing with the problems which press themselves on us.

All these "remnants" can be seen in reported facts which could be mentioned in connection with discussion of responsibility for the cold war and world tensions. But expectation conditioning has evidently influenced many leading thinkers in foreign policy to ignore them as a matter of course so they have little influence on ideas and opinion. If more questions were asked, they might have the impact and influence which might be warranted.

The Voice of America and Radio Free Europe may indeed be relics of the cold war but when it comes to relics, the U.S. and Western Europe are simply no match for the Soviet Union. It would seem to be a safe bet that if the Kremlin would discard its relics, the West would be glad to do the same. There would simply be no need to surmount obstacles to provide the people of Eastern Europe and Russia with information and news items which are taken for granted in many other parts of the world.

Another issue that influential people are determined not to discuss is the frequent convergence of U.S. and Soviet viewpoints at certain places. Have we become so convinced of our blame for tensions that we think we need to see things as Soviet criticism sees them? In the torrent of slogans over blame for tensions, it could be worthwhile to examine viewpoints which seem close to those of the Kremlin.

It is the Soviet view that U.S. troops should be withdrawn from Western Europe. This idea has had enough support in the U.S. to throw a good scare into our NATO allies. It was the Soviet view that the U.S. was meddling in the internal affairs of Russia by insistence on linking trade and credits with emigration. This view was certainly held by many influential people in the U.S. The Soviets have tried to persuade us that trade will lead to "better relations" between the U.S. and Russia. The idea certainly has wide support in the U.S. The Soviet Union would certainly like the American voting and opinion-polling public to believe that the U.S. is principally or solely to blame for world tensions (even as Soviet spokesmen insist that the "war of ideas" continues and must be officially encouraged). Many influential people in the U.S. will certainly agree that the U.S. is to blame for practically everything.

It is quite true that the Kremlin and some Americans wanted U.S. troops out of Europe for what were stated as different reasons. But the American public was simply tossed a few slogans about the "diminished threat" or the "needless expense" and these were supposed to answer all questions and settle the matter.

There was a conspicuous lack of awkward questions. Has the threat really diminished? Is it really too expensive to keep troops there? Has the long-run potential expense of unilaterally pulling troops out really been discussed? Although the clamor in the U.S. for withdrawing troops from Europe subsided somewhat after the final collapse in Vietnam, there was a time when many influential people were quite insistent.

One would think it might be worthwhile for influential thinkers in foreign policy to get together for public discussion on a few obvious questions. To what extent can we see things the way the Soviet Union and other adversaries want us to see them, without even discussing viewpoints publicly, and still protect our interests? To what extent can we see things the way they want us to on matters affecting the security of the Western alliance, such as U.S. troops in Western Europe?

It isn't just Americans who should raise the questions as to the extent to which they can see things the way the Soviets want the world to see them. The Soviets would like the world to believe, for example, that in any confrontation between any power and the Soviet Union, it is the responsibility of the other power to give way, in the interest of "peace" of course. The Russians would like this to be part of the general expectation conditioning which creates a favorable atmosphere for the application of political and military pressures far from Russian borders. The Soviets would like the world to believe that any effort to pry open the hermetically sealed confinement and isolation of the Soviet and satellite peoples, and suggestion as to "free movement of people and ideas" is "meddling in their internal affairs." Thus, any increase in tensions is obviously the fault of other countries. A surprising number of people and governments in countries which have expelled Soviet agents for meddling in their internal affairs, for subversion, espionage or sabotage, are willing to go along.

There are many examples of the expectation conditioning. There was supposed to have been progress on "mutual balanced force reductions" in Europe before the signing of the 1975 European security pact. This "linkage" was soon abandoned. In return for signatures on the pact it would apparently have been unthinkable to ask Russia for progress on troop reduction, to refrain from insisting on joint rule of the Spitzbergen Islands with Norway or to refrain from pouring money into Portugal for the specific purpose of meddling in the internal affairs of that country. This type of insistence would have questioned Russia's "right" to meddle in the internal affairs of other countries even as they were insisting no one had the "right" to meddle in Russia's internal affairs. Anyone who does insist on reciprocity would be challenging the expectation conditioning. Insistence on reciprocity would have questioned the time-honored double standard of conduct and no one would want to do that. It might offend "the Russians," the 5% ruling elite who speak and act for no one but themselves. Once again, the idea of reciprocity was overcome by the long-ingrained expectation conditioning.

The influential people seem determined not to talk publicly about whether our expectations in dealing with Russia have been conditioned. Perhaps they are afraid to raise such questions. Perhaps they are afraid of what the answers might be. Or perhaps they don't think events merit inquiry. They may believe there is nothing to be concerned about.

Apparently it is of no concern to any of the leading thinkers on foreign policy that when Soviet agriculture, industry or economy is in trouble, Western nations are "expected" to come to the rescue. They can be counted on to do it. When Western countries are in economic trouble, the Soviet Union encourages oil-producing nations to continue an oil embargo. The Soviets can be counted on to do their part. They are "expected" to do this.

But anyone who wonders out loud whether this is really the way détente is supposed to work is likely to be denounced as being against peace or in favor of tensions. Détente works very well for the Soviet system. Perhaps its chances of survival are better than the chances of the Western Alliance. We are "expected" to aid the survival of the Soviet system. The Soviet system is "expected" to seek the demise of NATO. If questions were asked, we might discover that the West is being psychologically conditioned not only against its own survival but in favor of the survival of the Soviet political and economic system. But there are no public questions. Only silence.

The Soviet Union feels free to meddle in the internal affairs of Portugal and other NATO members but timid voices in the U.S. and Western Europe caution against asking the free passage of people and ideas between East and West. The apparent psychological conditioning to this double standard and absence of reciprocity is as remarkable as it is appalling. We seem to have given up asking where we are or where we are going. The momentum appears to have been established and no one really dares to question it for fear of appearing to revive cold war issues. The momentum has been established and there is little sign that it is going to be affected. The motion will probably remain irreversible as long as efforts to discuss pertinent questions are considered a provocation, an act of deliberate impudence contrary to the spirit of "the current détente."

This is not to say that the questions raised here in any way demonstrate or prove that the United States or its allies aren't principally to blame or as much to blame as Russia for the cold war and world tensions. This is not to say that the questions raised here couldn't be answered to the complete satisfaction of the college professor or the man on the street. This is only to say that the advocates of the idea that the U.S. or the West is to blame, and the opponents of the idea, have not put their ideas and theories on the line for public questioning. They haven't gotten themselves and the public involved in trying to sort out the doctrines, opinions and slogans which are bandied about as if they were self-evident truths. Again, it is not a question of what information we have but what reported facts we use to see whether they can be reconciled with ideas, doctrines and slogans.

The need for such discussion should be obvious. If the American public is told that the U.S. is "perpetuating the cold war" when we are only trying to protect our interests, we obviously may fail to protect our interests. Conversely, if the American public is told that we are "protecting our interests" when in fact we may be "perpetuating the cold war," then U.S. policies may indeed be endangering international peace and security.

It should be readily apparent that the U.S. electorate may be in a position where it will need to decide just what the country is doing and decide whether to change or continue the policy. Is a given policy, which the public is asked to support, "protecting our interests" or "perpetuating the cold war"? The influential people ought to know this is a difficult choice and that making this choice is an important responsibility for the electorate to assume. The professors, politicians, experts and officials ought to know the American people need and deserve all the help they can get in making a duly considered judgment on these issues.

6

Escapes

When confronted with situations which suggest the individual has obligation to respond, there are two courses of action. The person can accept the responsibility to do what needs to be done or devise some means of escape from it.

If we can assume it is the individual's and the nation's responsibility to discuss issues, search for some common ground or consensus and at least be informed of where we are and where we are headed, there are various ways of avoiding this responsibility. The escapes from responsibility take many and varied forms.

The escapes from responsibility which we devise may or may not reflect our attitude toward society. We may really be willing to accept responsibility but find ourselves surrounded with readily available substitutes for responsibility which we are told do indeed represent our responsibility. They may be excuses for doing nothing, for doing something else which is easier than our responsibility but which is made to appear as if it were our responsibility.

The escapes from responsibility are confusing because they are rarely labelled as such. They are often billed as something that meets the responsibilities of citizenship, as some form of obligation. But again it seems unlikely that we can learn to recognize the escapes without discussing them and it appears that the professors, politicians, experts, officials and journalists will have to lead the way. But if the influential people are reluctant to discuss escapes they may need some prodding.

74

The influential people may have learned to rely on them as much as anyone else.

*　　*　　*

Systems of philosophy dealing with individual and collective responsibility have a long history. Attempts to systematize the individual's orientation in responsibility are many and varied. Some of these attempts may represent thinking and others may represent substitutes for thinking, something a person can do which may seem like a responsibility but is actually a substitute. Any system of thought which is applied to an individual's responsibility to his society must necessarily be examined in the light of the question as to whether reality is systematic. Can there be a systematic responsibility within a reality which is not systematic? Can reality be squeezed into, and interpreted in terms of, Hegel's dialectic? Can we really understand our responsibility in terms of the dialectic?

The long tradition of systematic thought in philosophy may reflect a strong feeling that whatever is difficult must be complex. It may be assumed that the problem of individual responsibility in society is so difficult that it therefore must be complex. It follows easily from this that therefore the most complicated systems of philosophy must be the ones best suited to the solution of difficult problems. It apparently doesn't seem possible that any "difficult" problem could also be "simple."

But this may be precisely the case. Our most difficult problems may really be very simple but our minds have been geared to complexity by the demands of civilization and technology. It often happens that the best technology is also the most complex, but not always. When confronted with a difficult problem of responsibility, there may be a tendency to "complexify" it by attempting to fit it into a complex system, apparently in the hope that this will make it more manageable. This may be done with problems which are not susceptible to complexification.

Perhaps it was no accident that Karl Marx chose Hegel's dialectic, about the most complicated system he could have found, to incorporate into his dialectical materialism as a means of explaining the economic phenomena he observed. It is almost as if he reasoned that if he was dealing with a difficult problem, a complicated system would be required to solve it. This may also explain the wide and durable appeal of Marxist theory. It probably would have been long forgotten if it had been simple. It would have been discounted as not being equal to the problem. It is considered almost inconceivable that the difficult choices we have to make may not be complicated but may instead be rather simple. If they are simple, it will be difficult ever to overcome the inertia of such a long period of indoctrination, of the expectation conditioning which equates complexity with difficulty.

This is not to suggest that asking whether statements can be reconciled with reported facts can or should be a substitute for all systematic thought, a substitute for the academic disciplines of philosophy or theology. This is merely to suggest that the study of academic theory should not become a refuge from the simple, difficult choices which aren't susceptible to resolution by systematic thought. This is merely to suggest that theory not become an escape from discussion on how we will be known to ourselves and others, what our choice of what is important will say about us, and whether we will adequately orient ourselves in the responsibilities demanded of us by the form of society and government we have inherited and claim to support. There may be some difficult choices which are also very simple, choices from which there can be no escape, no refuge in abstract theory.

The problem of evaluating an idea or slogan may not always be a complex one of trying to squeeze it into some doctrine or system of philosophy. It may be a very simple problem of asking whether the idea can be explained in terms of what everybody knows. This is not to say that reconciling slogans with reported facts, or seeing whether they can be reconciled, is easy. It may be, in fact, more difficult than a doctrinal or systematic approach because it is necessary to suspend the habit of approaching problems in the customary fashion. Forgetting doctrine and system, where required, may be the hardest task of all. Asking questions about the compatibility of statements and reports may offer resistance because it is too simple, both because of the way our minds are attuned and because of the conditioned expectation—what is difficult, it is thought, cannot be simple.

There may be some who will try systematic thought to try to find solutions to problems of individual responsibility and find that it doesn't work. Since systematic thought in philosophy for example, is so highly respected, a person could easily conclude that systematic philosophy is the best there is and if that doesn't work, one might as well give up. Some may be disappointed at failure to find an orientation in responsibility while others may be glad to have an excuse for giving up the quest on ground that doctrines and systems aren't for them. If systematic thought is the best there is, and it doesn't seem to work with unsystematic problems, what's the use?

* * *

If we ask questions we may find that there are not only doctrinal or systematic means of escaping or avoiding responsibility but also emotional means. Another means of avoiding the responsibility to ask and answer certain questions may be found in the time-honored ritual of public debate.

Debate as a substitute for the responsibility of evaluating ideas may be deceptive because it intends and purports to be a means of dealing with issues, becoming involved in problems, accepting responsibility.

To overcome the impulse to debate, it may be necessary to overcome two forces. One is the conditioned expectation that debate is a good way to deal with matters of deciding responsibility; the other force is that of instinct. To survive, to prevail, to vanquish and humiliate the challenger, all are instinctive. All these instincts are involved in the ritual of debate. Unfortunately, a popular way to evaluate ideas, to test them for validity, is to put them to the test of debate.

In practice, however, debate is more likely to be a test of the individuals participating than a test of the reliability of the ideas. Hardly anyone can isolate himself or herself from

77

the emotional and instinctive forces which invade and dominate nearly every public debate. A debate is more likely to settle the question of "who wins" than of "what is valid," of whether ideas we we rely on are in fact reliable.

People tend to "hang on" to their ideas and regard questioning or challenging as a personal attack, an act of hostility. Too often the objective in debate is to overcome the opponent, to destroy esteem and credibility. The instinct is that of self-preservation, the atmosphere is one in which only one contestant can survive; it is almost a gladiator arena, often with an audience to give emotional support to the more popular contestant, hardly the best setting for detached evaluation of ideas.

When discussing ideas, especially emotionally charged slogans, it is difficult to resist engaging in debate. It is difficult to overcome the "gladiator" and "survival" instinct involving ego and esteem. It is difficult to resist the temptation to try to come out on top in an argument. It is very hard to impute honorable motives to one who honestly questions a popular idea or one's favorite slogans. It is easy to assume that a person who asks such questions or makes such challenges is out to "get" someone or other. It is difficult, in other words, to maintain an atmosphere in which there is disinterested, detached discussion in which it can be asked whether ideas we rely on merit trust in them, whether certain ideas, slogans and statements will stand questioning, can be explained.

However, the creation of this atmosphere, the atmosphere of inquiry, in which curiosity may have a free rein, is a very simple act of will and discipline. It requires overcoming certain instincts, reflexes, suspicions and other habits of thought. It requires restraining feelings and reserving judgment until questions have been asked and answered, to provide the atmosphere conducive to inquiry, to the free questioning which alone can determine whether a statement can be explained in the light of reported facts. What is required, in other words, is an act of will which is very simple, very unsystematic and very difficult. In fact, it would probably be easier to do something systematic and complicated.

Thus, the ability to solve difficult but simple problems of evaluating ideas may rest not on the ability to master complex doctrines and systems of thought but rather to suspend systematic thinking, to suspend the primitive instinct to overpower an opponent, to suspend suspicion of motives and overcome the assumption that an honest challenge is hostile. The ability to evaluate ideas may depend, in other words, on the ability to do unaccustomed things, to resist the temptation to overcomplicate, to do some very simple but very difficult things. We thrive on complexity. Simplicity, being forgotten and unfamiliar, is our pitfall.

Thus, there is not only the systematic escape but the emotional escape. The heat of the debate is a handy excuse for not asking questions to understand what certain doctrines and slogans might mean. Debate seems to be a handy excuse for not giving curiosity a free rein because it seems to be the most acceptable format we have for evaluating ideas, especially those associated with national politics or policy. But an "acceptable," "time-honored," widely used, "everybody does it" escape is still an escape from the responsibility we must meet, from what our system of society and government demands of us.

* * *

If there were public discussion in effort to answer certain questions, we might find there are many doctrines which express wishful thinking. For example, we might find that the doctrine that the U.S. is to blame for world tensions and many of the other ills besetting humanity may be a form of wishful thinking. It may represent the hope that everything which is wrong is the fault of the U.S. because the U.S. has been known to change policies, in Vietnam for example, while Soviet policies tend to remain constant, as in Vietnam, for example. There may be a general resignation to the reality that it is no use to appeal to Russia or to other authoritarian powers to change their external policies in any significant and permanent measure. The only hope, then, is to get the U.S. to change policies.

The statements that most of what is wrong in the world

79

is the fault of the U.S. may express the hope that it is so. It may express the hope that we live in such a pleasant, simple, secure world that we can unilaterally fix everything all by ourselves. This hope, if these assumptions have merit, easily becomes the admonition for the U.S. to remedy what is wrong by changing policies, while refraining from similar admonitions to the Soviet Union or other powers which aren't always innocent bystanders when there is a crisis to be exploited. The apparent hope that the U.S. is solely to blame for conflicts such as Vietnam, the wishful thinking that it is exclusively our fault, easily becomes translated into a demand that the U.S. do something to stop it. There is no use asking Russia to restrain its allies. It is up to us to restrain ours.

If what is wrong in the world is generally, mostly or totally the fault of the U.S., the problems confronting U.S. citizens representing the general public, the lawmakers and other influential people, are greatly simplified. All we have to do is change our policies and everything will be all right. War in Vietnam? We can change that. And we do. Confrontation with Russia? We can change that. And we do. We don't ask the Russians to change that. It is all very simple and it avoids awkward questions which might lead to hard choices. But it may be wishful thinking. We may have to acknowledge that some things that go wrong aren't our fault and we may have to maintain policies or make hazardous efforts to persuade other great powers to change theirs.

Partly as a result of the expectation conditioning which often prevails over a spirit of inquiry, it has become fashionable among Americans to be quick to blame the U.S. for various ills of the world. It makes these people appear reasonable and fair-minded, willing to reserve judgment on everyone but themselves. However, in many cases this may be wishful thinking and, as such, irresponsible.

It would be a great easing of our political burdens if we could simply stop opposing what other powers are doing. We could avoid fatiguing tensions and hard choices. We could simply pull away whenever there is a threat or confrontation. But this is probably too easy a solution.

If we could get some public discussion by experts on the subject we might find that there will be times when we will have to declare that the conflicts of the world are not all our fault, that we will have to stand firm. We may simply have to resign ourselves to making judgments of individual cases, sorting out those situations which are our fault from those which are not, even though this has become unfashionable among many of the professors, politicians, experts, officials and journalists. We may have to endure the doubts and tensions which are involved in all hard choices. This country wasn't founded on wishful thinking and easy choices. There is no reason to assume it can survive and function on them.

There are many reasons to avoid reliance on wishful thinking which are sufficient in themselves. Another reason which would independently justify rejecting wishful thinking is the preservation of intellectual honesty. Can we really be intellectually honest if we allow wishful thinking to prevent us from taking well-known reported facts into account when making decisions? If a favored idea and a reported fact can't be reconciled, if they are incompatible in the mind, intellectual honesty and integrity demand choosing one or the other, where a choice must be made. The alternative is to invite disorientation, the weakness of confusion and indecision. It is because of the basic necessity to avoid unnecessary confusion that intellectual honesty becomes more of a necessity than a virtue. To a great extent, we can learn and continue to take adequate note of circumstances, continue to function effectively and appropriately only if we retain a certain degree of intellectual honesty. Escape into wishful thinking may be a burden not only because of the consequences in our actions but because of the way we feel about it, the disorientation and discouragement it may produce.

If we claim to be concerned about the "moral climate" in the United States, we have to ask whether we are being deceived or are deceiving ourselves. Perhaps we need to extend the concept of "honesty" beyond the basic requirements of not cheating or lying. If we hear ideas which need to be explained and which are not explained and let them pass without question, are we being intellectually honest? Perhaps we can pass the test of honesty in the usually understood sense by not cheating, stealing or lying. However, intellectual honesty may require more of us. In order to be intellectually honest, it may be necessary to ask questions about what we don't understand, about what hasn't been explained. To be intellectually honest and responsible is to exercise simple, ordinary curiosity, to ask obvious questions which suggest themselves, to follow wherever curiosity leads except where there is some unwarranted intrusion.

If we accept what has been publicly stated and hasn't been publicly explained, the issue goes beyond honesty and responsibility. The issue becomes our willingness to face reality. Perhaps the moral climate of a country can't really be separated from the willingness of leaders, with the backing of citizens, to face reality, to shun escapes from it as being unworthy. If we accept ideas which haven't been explained and perhaps can't be explained, we are turning away from reality, ceasing to function as self-governing people, giving up, drifting on slogans. The silence on the question of what we are doing may represent one of the escapes.

We may have to discuss and consider the possibility that it may be the individual's responsibility not to let curiosity be shut off, but to keep asking questions about what hasn't been explained. However, the honesty of curiosity is, in our sophisticated world, associated with naivete and childishness. Children ask honest, awkward questions because they don't know any better. It is an annoying habit they will outgrow when they are older and more mature. We are all born with honest curiosity but most people learn there are certain rewards for not rocking the boat, for learning not to ask questions, for not breaking The Rules. Responsibility may involve declining these rewards and persisting in questioning. Perhaps curiosity will come back in vogue if we begin to associate questioning with necessary awareness, and necessary awareness with survival of our form of government. But for the time being most influential people have learned to escape to the refuge of silence.

Why exercise curiosity, why ask questions about what hasn't been explained? Without persistent efforts to monitor and evaluate ideas, there can be a degree of intellectual anarchy even among self-governing people. Intellectual anarchy can lead to political chaos in what was formerly a democracy.

Intellectual anarchy can occur when there is no dialogue, no attempt to control, question or evaluate a stampede of slogans. They assume a life and energy of their own, run wild, out of control, with no fear of challenge, causing oblivion of reported facts with attending disorientation, with attending artificial confusion and conflict. Their momentum changes public opinion even when the reported facts of the situation remain the same. In Vietnam, for example, we were supporting one dictator or another from the beginning of our involvement, with the possible exception of Diem in 1963. Yet public opinion was "changed" from "supporting an ally" to "supporting a dictator." This ability to think independently of reported facts can usually be traced to slogans with a life and will of their own. Many of the slogans reflect acknowledgment of some facts but not others, or reflect the acknowledgment of different reported facts at different times, even when the reports have remained consistent. It may be that selecting only the facts we like leads to intellectual anarchy just as obeying only the laws we like can lead to political anarchy.

Another means of escape from discussion of what our responsibilities in the world might be could be called thinking small. For some people, it is silly even to discuss the idea that the U.S. should continue to play the role of one of the superpowers in the world.

It is quite true that we didn't really ask to be the sole effective counterweight to Soviet power. But this is the way it turned out from the consequences of two world wars, neither of which was started by the U.S. and from which the U.S. emerged with its economic and military power intact. We obviously don't relish this role and many of us would like to pass the buck to someone else if we could find any takers. We didn't ask for this role but history has a way of

83

being arbitrary and capricious and we appear to be saddled with superpower status for the time being.

Some influential people will insist that we ardently sought this position in world affairs which makes us appear as defender of the status quo and therefore has the effect of making us the consistent frontrunner as international scapegoat. Some will insist we eagerly sought this role and can therefore drop it, that we can leave a vacuum with no ill effects or that someone will step in to fill the empty space. There are some who apply the term "pax Americana" to our efforts to exert influence or control over events outside our borders or beyond Western Europe. Some would apparently like us to return to a peaceful, pastoral, primitive, innocent existence we haven't enjoyed for many years, if we ever did. Sound arguments could be made that Americans in general are temperamentally unsuited to the role we are playing on the world stage. Thinking small would be a tempting escape.

If influential people were discussing questions which might be discussed, we might find that many of our slogans over recent years have been less anti-war than pro-utopia. They seem to express the hope that we can withdraw from untidy entanglements with unpleasant foreigners and build our own perfect society on our own private Olympus of peace and freedom and democracy. Much of the recent "no-disturbance" foreign policy seems to express the hope that we are not really a major power or that if we are, we can be the only major power not involved in world affairs. It may very well be that we don't need to worry about the balance of power, about defense treaty obligations outside NATO or Japan, about dealing with thrusts of other great powers in areas which are geographically awkward and politically inconvenient. It may very well be that if only we will be friendly and agreeable and reduce money spent on armaments, other powers will find they have no choice but to do the same. But the professors, politicians, experts and officials certainly ought to give us some public discussion about it. Are we trying to think small? Can we afford to think small? We may be taking a fundamentally escapist attitude if we believe we live in a world that doesn't make demands of us.

* * *

Is it possible that we are too polite to understand each other? It may be that the influential people who have discussions with each other exercise excessive politeness. As long as a question is asked courteously and with an honest desire to understand whether an idea can be explained, the question shouldn't be considered impolite. It should not be considered impolite merely because the person asked may prefer not to answer that particular kind of question. If asking to understand how statements and reports can exist side by side is impolite, we need a more sensible definition of politeness, one that will enable us to sustain our system of society and government. Without a better definition of politeness, we will have to resign ourselves to never understanding what some of the influential people are telling us.

If we are too polite to ask awkward, obvious questions, to give a free rein to curiosity, to go wherever questioning reasonably leads, to ask to understand ideas and slogans which guide our decisions, it may turn out that we are too polite to sustain our form of government. If we are afraid of giving offense when we ask to understand the ideas we are urged to accept as guiding assumptions, too polite to get explanations of slogans which determine our actions in answering obligations and exercising our rights in self-government, we may turn out to be too polite to survive.

It would indeed be ironic if we managed to emerge intact from a successful revolution, a series of subsequent challenges including two world wars and two non-wars, a modern exodus of draft-age young men, the Watergate fiasco, the CIA scandals and miscellaneous calamities too numerous to mention, only to find that we are too infernally polite to ask our politicians, professors and experts to explain what they are saying. It would be tragic if we allowed our opinions to be guided by slogans which are substitutes for thinking just because everybody is so painfully polite that we can't get clear on what we are doing and where we are going. If we

85

are too courteous to ask how slogans can be explained and where they are taking us, we won't keep our form of government nor will we deserve to. The historic record tends to show that people who want to be self-governing have to deserve to be self-governing.

We are not only too polite to each other, we are too polite to our allies, our adversaries and everyone in between. We are too polite to insist that other countries live up to explicit or implicit understandings. We are too polite to insist that the Soviet Union live up to written or tacit agreements or understandings for cooperation in Indochina or the Middle East in support of "détente." We are too polite to confront allies and make an issue of steps they are taking to accelerate the proliferation of nuclear weapons among third world nations. We baffle and confuse everyone by boasting of our military power and then acting like scared rabbits when it comes to compelling compliance with agreements or understandings which would seem essential to avoid consequences which could lead to nuclear war. This inconsistency can only lead to miscalculations and unintended confrontations. If we appear to be retreating and suddenly find we have to turn and draw the line, someone may step over out of sheer momentum. It may not even be intentional. We could have nuclear extermination by mistake. There is such danger in a course which persists in overpoliteness until it may become necessary to suddenly and unexpectedly hold firm.

We are sometimes so polite we make ourselves look weak and lacking in resolve. If our outer defenses and inner institutions crumble under politeness, we are polite to the point of being uncivilized, to the point of jeopardizing our civilization. If we are so polite we fail to draw lines and make clear our intentions and interests, our politeness in a nuclear age becomes a menace to ourselves and to the rest of the world.

This chronic national epidemic of politeness to the point of paralysis may be traceable to the influential people. They seem to be afraid of giving offense by asking simple, obvious, awkward, uncomfortable questions. It is an attitude which appears to manifest itself in our domestic and foreign policy.

To a person lacking in expertise it may easily appear that we fail to make clear what we will and will not do, what we will and will not tolerate from adversaries and what we will or will not expect of allies.

As might be expected, there is a complete lack of discussion among leading thinkers as to whether our overpoliteness may be a means of escape from responsibility. Overpoliteness could be serving as an excuse for following The Rules, as an excuse for keeping silent when questions ought to be raised.

*   *   *

Generally speaking, the success of a representative form of government depends on how important it is to those who govern and are governed by their representatives. Generally speaking, representative government requires a certain amount of attention and it continues to function only as long as it is important enough to receive this minimum amount of effort and attention.

Why do we need to discuss what is important in connection with our responsibilities? Whether we succeed as a self-governing people will depend on what we decide is important, on whether we will take time to evaluate ideas in public discussion and ponder the evaluations amid all the forces which compete for our attention and energy. It will depend on whether discussions about slogans, and their reliability, can find a place amid social, financial and political competition, amid the enticing diversions which accompany the rewards of such competition. In other words, will we find time to make the choices and decisions required of us?

For the ordinary citizen, in many cases, the escape from responsibility is made easy by the overwhelming competition of other matters and the demands made by business-related social activity. The most common and readily available escape from the demands of our social and political system is the 18-hour work day. But it is generally considered bad form to acknowledge that business takes precedence over all else. A man won't usually admit that business is more important than his family or his responsibilities as a citizen, even when actions indicate rather clearly that business comes first. Frequent efforts to deny what actions show, however, suggest that people are aware of what is important, or what ought to be, even if their lives deny it.

To what extent does our system of "escapes" in avoiding discussion affect us and our domestic and foreign policy? Is there a difference between what is important to us judging from actions and what we say or pretend is important? Are influential people asking about what actions and situations, events and circumstances, tell about what Americans think is important? Influential people are often reluctant to ask about the refinements of deception and coercion, the civilized infighting, the double standard, the pretense of valuing people and reality of valuing financial, social or political ascendancy.

There may be an embarrassing disparity between what we know or suspect ought to be important to us and what our actions show is important. Discussion involving the public might bring this out, might enable us to see ourselves all too clearly. But understanding what our form of government requires of us may involve a certain amount of embarrassment if discussion should indicate that we aren't living up to expectations. Understanding of what is required, and how close we are to measuring up, may be essential. It is certainly to be hoped that we aren't going to permit possible embarrassment to keep us from doing what is required.

There may be discrepancies between what we profess to value and what actions and circumstances show we value. In other times this would have been called hypocrisy but the descriptive terms applied today are more scientific, more precise, less subjective and above all, less embarrassing. But these modern expressions and explanations may only be a convenient refuge, one of the many handy escapes.

We have to decide, and have some means of deciding, whether we are going to accept responsibility or escape it. We have to decide whether we are going to solve problems or find alternatives which may amount to adjusting to problems instead. If there were discussion, questions and answers, we might find that we are erecting mechanisms which function to protect people from facing what is involved in being self-governing.

Whether we succeed in preserving our form of government may depend on an understanding of any differences between what we say or pretend is important and what our routine actions show is important. Our values may turn out to be perfectly in order and self-evidently beyond question but perhaps we shouldn't merely assume this without public discussion by intellectual leaders in various disciplines. Or perhaps our values are totally out of line with our national objectives and with the demands of the form of government we are trying to preserve. But no conclusion, or even an estimate, can be made without discussion. In other words, without discussion we are drifting.

Without discussion we are drifting because without discussion we are without knowledge of where we are, let alone where we want to go. Steering our course requires that we know our position as well as our destination.

It is quite true that we can never reach agreement on where we are, where we want to go, what we value in our words and what we value in our actions and whether there is a difference. We can never hope to agree on what is important and what ought to be. But is this a valid reason for not discussing directions and values? We may be able to reach a consensus, if not agreement. Even if there is no consensus, discussion of values, of what is important, could lead to a better public understanding of needed directions and more effective and intelligent efforts in political activity on behalf of candidates and causes.

Perhaps the fundamental question is rather simple. Are our responsibilities to our social and political institutions important enough so that we will give up the escapes?

7

Rewards

There can be little doubt that interaction of people of differing views, in public discussion, would place an added burden on the influential people who currently confine their activities to writing and speaking, with only a negligible amount of asking and answering questions. Such interaction of influential people would also involve additional effort on the part of the general public. They would have to follow the discussion on subjects such as détente in order to know whether to support or oppose such a policy when they have the opportunity. Would the extra effort be worthwhile? Would there be rewards?

The answer to this question depends on further questions. First we need to ask whether lack of public discussion of certain issues is what is wrong with our system. Then we have to ask whether the effort involved, the self-education necessary, to make our system work better is worth the effort, whether the rewards are commensurate with the demands.

One of the rewards of interaction of people of differing views would simply be to establish communication among people who seem to shun all contact with each other. When there is public discussion, it seems, political liberals generally talk with each other, as do political conservatives. Any discussion between liberals and conservatives seems to be against The Rules. There seems to be a lack of interaction where it would seem to be desirable and appropriate.

If there were interaction between people of differing views, there could be definite rewards. If they would engage in discussion, we might even find out how opposite conclusions are reached from what is presumably the same set of reported facts. The first discovery we might make is whether there is, or can be, agreement as to what reported facts are. Are differences based on different perceptions of reported facts or on differing conclusions from agreed upon facts?

It may be that some professors, politicians, experts and officials simply leave certain reports out of account when reaching their conclusions. If so, the obvious question is, why? One set of facts agreed on by all responsible news media reporting independently of each other. Opposite conclusions from these reports. The fact that no one is asking questions about what would seem worth discussing shows the lack of curiosity among influential people.

Is it possible that opposite views can flow from the same set of reports? How? Why? Is it of no concern to the leading thinkers that one conclusion may be more justified than the other and that it might be wise to find out which? When one conclusion might lead us to success and the other to blunder and catastrophe, is it of no consequence which is which? Isn't it worthwhile to find out? Wouldn't there be rewards if we can learn to avoid certain errors?

If two people with differing views accept and understand reported facts in different ways, it would seem worthwhile to direct questions toward the reason for this. How can the same set of reports be understood in different ways, so that there are separate starting places toward the separate conclusions. Can we allow prejudgments or predisposition to lead us to conclusions which can't be explained in terms of reported news accounts?

If two people with differing views accept and understand reported facts in the same way, a reasonable procedure might be to determine how they reach opposite conclusions from the same starting place. Certainly the public discussion on this question wouldn't lead to agreement that one doctrine or the other represents self-evident truth. But it is possible that where opposite views are drawn from the same set of facts, the more often repeated view may either be affirmed or upset by questions and answers, by following where curiosity leads. It may happen that after careful discussion, the argument or slogan which at first seemed weaker will appear more reasonable and more explicable than one which had been more widely accepted.

If taking care to rely only on ideas and statements which can be explained in terms of what most people know will help us avoid only a few large or medium-size errors in running our society and government, this will be the reward for the effort by the influential people and the general public.

Opposing views based on the same set of facts would seem to be sufficient reason for, and a natural starting place for, public discussion by influential people. The opposing views should be, in other words, an intellectual provocation and stimulus, something that should be discussed, something that should not stand unattended, something that should be investigated. However, few influential thinkers see fit to accept the challenge posed by these provocations. It is easier to write books and articles and give lectures.

It is possible that by determining which of two opposing views is more readily explanable we may be able, for example, to avoid reliving history. This repetition is not only monotonous but dangerous. As weapons become more and more formidable, it becomes more urgent to find a means of avoiding cyclical patterns in history.

Discussion may be our only means of controlling the repetition of events. If the repetition of unpleasant events is caused by repetition of uncontrolled slogans, it will be necessary to learn to use discussion to restrain slogans. It may not be oversimplification to say that we will have to decide whether we will control slogans or whether they will control us. During crisis periods, they seem to get the upper hand with menacing regularity and persuade us to do what we later come to regret, and indeed may agree was unnecessary.

The rights we enjoy were not established by people who had a habit of taking refuge from awkward, difficult issues. The hope that we can preserve our social and political system while we insist on avoiding discussion of reported facts which may interfere with slogans is itself an example of escapism.

As long as the American public in general and the influential people in particular fail to engage in public dialogue on whether widely accepted statements can be reconciled with reported facts, Americans are acting as if someone other than Americans holds responsibility for our fate, as if we aren't really a self-governing people and don't really have ultimate responsibility for shaping domestic and foreign policy. Allowing slogans to shape these responsibilities is like turning part of our responsibility over to someone else who is in no way answerable. The reward for keeping our system in our hands is a better functioning of that system.

The American people, like it or not, are finally responsible for solving or for judging solutions to problems of American policy. We can properly solve these problems or properly judge solutions offered by representatives only if we can shake off our reluctance to talk about the problems, to try to evaluate ideas and slogans which are offered as solutions but which may prove to be substitutes for solutions and substitutes for thinking. Whether we are too lazy, too polite, too afraid or too busy to have these discussions, the result is the same. We drift. The reward for necessary public discussion, and for the effort involved for all, would be to reassert our ability to steer our course among the pitfalls which wait in our path.

In avoiding difficult questions about widely accepted assumptions, some of them our guiding assumptions on national policy, we are disengaged not only from our responsibilities but from each other. By protecting our slogans and assumptions from awkward, nagging questions, we only become more isolated from our political process and from each other. There is no discussion aimed at testing our guiding assumptions. Discussing or debating only what is easy, pleasant or familiar, we fail to use our freedom and exercise our responsibility. Fear of raising awkward and difficult questions is fear of what protects our rights. Individual rights under a system of laws always go together with awkward questions. We can't have one without the other. When questions stop, trouble starts.

There are at least two kinds of influential people. There is the kind of influential person who challenges widely accepted notions, who goes against the current when it is necessary, in an effort to persuade people to think. There is also the influential person who invents or repeats ideas in the form of slogans, who urges acceptance of substitutes for thinking, who in effect persuades people not to think. This may be done by urging acceptance of substitutes for questions and answers as to whether ideas can be explained. In the United States, and probably in the rest of the world as well, we seem to have a shortage of the former and an abundance of the latter.

Influential people could be accepting the responsibility to discuss and evaluate ideas and slogans we are urged to accept. They could be providing the intellectual stimulus and political leadership our form of government requires. They could be discussing underlying assumptions on which public opinion and national policies rest. They could be helping Americans and other independent peoples find areas of agreement so their clumsy systems can devise some means of meeting the challenges posed by systems of thought-control and minority rule. The rewards to all concerned would seem to be obvious.

When professors, politicians, experts and officials withdraw into books, articles and polite, perfunctory interviews, the layman may be justified in wondering whether he has been abandoned. Influential people often seem more interested in impressing each other than enlightening the general public. Certainly there must be scholarly books and articles intended for those who "speak the language," who are trained in certain disciplines. But a strong case could be made that there should also be more printed or broadcast presentations aimed at greater involvement of those who ultimately determine and who must ultimately be answerable for American domestic and foreign policy.

Perhaps the influential people who refuse to talk with each other and at the same time predict a dark future for the country or for the idea of democracy are creating a self-fulfilling prophecy. They refuse to discuss the statements, ideas and slogans which randomly influence opinion on national policies and then when slogans steer us into a bog, they say, "I told you so." Predicting that things will go badly is easier than asking and answering questions on national policy in public so that we can all educate ourselves to avoid mistakes. The silence which stifles discussion of national directions practically guarantees that things won't go better. People who ultimately must decide are being told, in effect, they shouldn't be in on discussion, shouldn't hear how facts are used in support of one point of view or the other. The rewards of public discussion would be a change in this situation and a better functioning of our system.

If we have questions and answers about the slogans which are likely to be revived in the next crisis, we will be prepared for that crisis. Vietnam probably demonstrated that it is very difficult to evaluate slogans in the heat of pressure and conflict. The time to discuss the recurring slogans is between conflicts so that we will not be ambushed by them every time there is a serious situation involving serious dispute.

If there were more interaction of influential people, more discussion of differing or opposing views for the benefit of the public, we might see many changes which would eventually benefit our understanding of our orientation in responsibility toward our system of society and government. For example, honesty might even become respectable again.

Among some people it has become fashionable to think of honesty as being out of style, foolish, impractical in a fast-moving society, something we can no longer afford if we are to continue our wheeling and dealing as usual. However, if there were discussion on the subject it might turn out that a certain amount of honesty is needed, as a practical matter, to make society and government function. It may even turn out that confidence among people is essential to the functioning of government and society and that honesty is essential to confidence.

We have seen certain phases of our government and society working poorly in recent years. It might be well to inquire just what role a lack of confidence and honesty had in these malfunctions. Would these breakdowns have occurred if there had been honesty and confidence? Why, according to recent opinion polls, is public esteem as regards the Presidency, Congress, the judiciary, the CIA and FBI so near all-time lows? Can we afford lack of confidence in our agencies and institutions? Can we afford not to have the honesty and candor which can maintain confidence and cooperation between representatives and those they represent, between officials and those they serve?

There might be good reason to reconsider what seems to be a popular belief that being honest is something that only saints or hermits can afford, that honesty isn't practical for ordinary people who have to have social, business and political dealings in today's world of fast and loose corner-cutting. Perhaps we need to rehabilitate the "image" of honesty from an unworkable abstraction for fuzzy thinkers to a real necessity in the functioning of our government and society. Painful and disillusioning as it may be for some, honesty and its effects may have genuine benefits and rewards in our government and society.

Someday we are going to learn that honesty is necessary to the functioning of our form of government and society. Some arrangements among people have always required a certain amount of trust if the arrangements are to continue. Some transactions among people can take place only in an atmosphere of confidence. Business dealings, and therefore the economy, are dependent on a certain level of confidence between buyer and seller. Someday we will learn that our political structure must lean on the same confidence. The only question is whether we will discover this before or after we allow it to fall apart.

If we are resolved to learn something from our past experience, through discussion of situations and the lessons to be learned, we may learn the lessons in time. If we are determined to have no discussion of experience, if we are determined to learn nothing from Watergate, nothing from the CIA and FBI scandals of recent years, we will learn the lesson too late.

There seems to be a tacit agreement among politicians,

professors, officials and experts that they won't ask each other to explain what they say on sensitive (and therefore important) issues of domestic and foreign policy. However, there is no such agreement among scientists, for example, or among physicians or psychologists. They are expected to explain what they say when offering a doctrine or theory. This paradox may explain why science is in the space age and why politics, for the most part, is still in the Stone Age. This may explain why Harvard-educated politicians are still hitting each other over the head with the most crude and clumsy stone-ax slogans and epithets. If scientists relied on doctrine and slogan to the extent politicians do, we would still be waiting for the wheel to be invented. There may be an inherent danger in trying to proceed with our peculiar predicament of having our weapons in the nuclear age and our politics handed down from Neanderthals.

One of the rewards of discussion in public among people of differing views might be to find alternatives to slogans and epithets, to find ways of questioning ideas instead of attacking advocates of those ideas in a manner which generates hostility. It could only be to our advantage to try to bring our means of evaluating ideas up to within a thousand years of our technology.

It is difficult to assess the silence of the influential people. It is as if they are unwilling to point out that other people's statements can't be reconciled with reported facts because somebody might do the same to them. Perhaps it is something no one wants to start. If it ever got started, nothing would be safe from revision or destruction if it couldn't be explained. Nothing would be sacred. Respected greybeard slogans could lose their status, their social acceptability. They could no longer serve as substitutes for thinking. Every slogan would be suspect. Ideas might have to be discarded before replacements could be found and replacements could be slow in coming. So many things would be uncertain. In other words, everything would be as it should be and as mature, responsible adults should expect it to be in the absence of comfortable slogans.

8

What Can We Do?

What if the influential people fail to offer public discussion to facilitate our involvement in deciding issues that affect us? What can we do? Any proposal to deal with social or political problems should answer the question, "What can we do?" It should have a workable answer for all members of the community, not just the influential people. How do we assert our rights of self-government?

There may be no ready-made apparatus which permits the person without "influence" to try to push or block certain trends or ideas, to make use of the small measure of political clout each citizen has been granted in our system. It is possible to have a "democratic" or a "representative" system of government without having a democratic process. If people don't *use* a "democratic" system, they are *acting as if* they are governed by some other kind of system.

It often appears that the "insider" officials in government don't want to give the "outsider" press and general public a chance to register support or opposition toward certain ideas or doctrines or policies because, it is thought, the public wouldn't understand or shouldn't get involved. Public discussion of domestic and foreign policy issues by influential people would allow public reaction to discussion to be recorded by the many pulse-takers in our system. There is never any shortage of opinion polls in the United States.

The voting and opinion-polled public can hardly give or withhold consent to such things as details of SALT agreements but the public must be satisfied with broad concepts such as détente with Russia if such ideas are to control national policy for any length of time. Those who wrote our Constitution arranged it that way. The need for our consent to general concepts of policy is a need our politicians sometimes try to ignore. Because of this need, the public should be involved as an audience in public discussion, toward helping to decide whether détente and other broad policy concepts should be pushed or blocked.

If self-governing people find themselves continually torn between opposing viewpoints with no discussion to reconcile the views with reported facts or with other views, what then? If we decide this isn't an acceptable state of affairs, what can be done? If self-governing people feel left out of a process they are entitled to be part of, what can be done? For one thing, we can tell the influential scholars, senators and other experts to change their attitudes toward their manner of presenting issues to the public:

1. A change of habit would be needed. Those in the habit of publicly expressing opinions would also get used to discussing them publicly, even with people who hold opposing views.

2. A new attitude toward "rights" would be needed. The right of free speech, expressing opinions, would presuppose the responsibility to ask and answer questions about opinions, as the other half of the right of free speech.

3. A change of attitude toward dialogue would be needed. Dialogue would become as important as monologue (such as a newspaper "opinion" column) as a means of aiding public understanding of issues in elections and in initiatives and referendums affecting domestic and foreign policy.

4. Fresh thinking is required about what self-governing people need in order to orient themselves in policy issues. These needs would be deemed to include not only reported facts (news) and "expert" opinion but also discussion of opinions in relation to each other and in relation to reported facts.

99

More specifically, the public can insist that those in position to influence public opinion do certain things they aren't doing now. For example:

1. Tell congressmen, governors, mayors, scholars, and their critics, to join in public discussion. Tell these people to involve each other and the public in discussion of issues the public must understand. Tell all these people that in addition to writing, speaking and lecturing they should give us dialogue to test ideas we may be relying on as guiding assumptions in national policy.

2. Urge radio and television broadcasters and newspaper and magazine publishers to invite influential people to take part in dialogue (not debate) for the purpose of helping the public understand issues and options available in domestic and foreign policy. There is no obvious reason why publishers and broadcasters can't call for dialogue on opposing views and give us the result in print and on the air. It should cease to be unthinkable.

3. Urge Common Cause and other good government groups, intended to represent the public interest, to arrange public discussion. Ask them to give us discussion which will give a basis for judgment of issues so polls and elections can give us a means of getting behind certain ideas or efforts when officials fail to make a move. There is no obvious reason why these groups can't work with publishers and broadcasters in persuading the officials and scholars to discuss issues, to give us questions and answers. We can no longer afford to dismiss such dialogues as unthinkable.

It is not being implied here that elected or appointed officials need to be guided by the current, fashionable public opinion. Public officials have made unpopular moves and have later been vindicated in their judgment or have succeeded in persuading the public the actions were correct. This is only to say that the general public's rights and responsibilities in the formation of policy need to be accorded more recognition and that public discussion is one possible means to that end.

If public urgings to those in positions of influence are greeted with less than enthusiasm, a distinct possibility, the public, the press, the broadcasters, the good government groups can ask the influential people a few direct questions. For example:

1. Are they putting caution ahead of responsibility, ahead of the needs of the country? Are they more concerned over how they might look explaining their own ideas than with giving us dialogue and guidance? Are they more concerned about their image than about their responsibilities?

2. How much longer can we fail to get explanations of opinions and guiding assumptions, fail to see whether we understand the ideas we may be relying on?

3. Why not make full use of free speech to serve our system?

4. Should we be satisfied with pairs of opposing views which reach a wide audience without discussion for the same wide audience?

5. Why not publicly discuss broad concepts for the information and benefit of those who must finally approve or reject them?

6. Should influential people explain what they say? Should other influential people ask them to explain?

7. Should we find out whether often-repeated and widely accepted statements can be explained in terms of reported facts?

8. Does their silence say everything is settled, there is no need for public discussion of controversial issues? If so, do they really mean to say this?

9. Are they assuming it is more trouble to have discussion and test ideas and steer our course than it is to

101

drift into mistakes on untested slogans?

10. Are they assuming issues that have been written about for decades aren't worth talking about?

11. Are they ignoring us and our role in government? Are they excluding us from the process? Wouldn't public discussion serve to include us in the process? Do they have suggestions for better ways to include us?

12. Is it possible for us to be a self-governing people without being involved in the process of government?

13. Are they going to use all of the right of free speech or just one easy, comfortable corner of it?

14. Why shouldn't dialogue be as much a part of our political experience as it is a part of our family, social and business experience?

We have an entire class of people who serve the public and who never have to explain anything to anyone's satisfaction except their own. Their standards may tend to be lax. Perhaps we should expect problems in domestic and foreign policy until the influential people have to explain statements to the satisfaction of the public. Corporation officers have to explain policies at meetings of stockholders. Perhaps we need to think of ourselves as the stockholders of the republic, entitled to hear public officials explain ideas and policies to each other and to us. Perhaps we need to think of ourselves as an audience which can give or withhold approval, as an audience with a legitimate interest.

We need a public state of mind that demands explanations of what hasn't been explained. It isn't a question of whether we have the best possible system of government. It is a question of whether our thought and action support the system we have.

We have a system, it appears, which runs on questions, which depends on ideas being questioned and challenged so we won't rely on untested notions that can steer us into a bog.

Unless we understand and *act as if* we understand what our system demands of us, we may look around some day and find we don't recognize the shambles we have made of what our founders entrusted to us.

We have a political system in which some policy decisions are thrust on us whether we are ready or not and whether we like it or not. After the candidates and experts have had their say, self-governing people need ways to make reliable judgments on certain matters of national policy. If policy matters are becoming more complex, this could mean new demands on self-governing people. We may need new methods to meet new demands. If we try to rely on old ways, on The Rules, on the monologue system, we may be saying, in effect, that we have given up on our system.

If we say, in effect, that discussion of the increasingly complex matters the public must understand is too difficult, we may be saying that self-government is too difficult. We may be saying that we are going to have to resign ourselves to accepting some other kind of system. To understand issues, we need to get involved in public dialogue. In the area of self-government, not getting involved can be the same as giving up.

Perhaps most troubling of all is that we aren't making any public inquiry into the question of whether we are doing what we need to do to sustain our form of government. We have no significant public dialogue on this question. Self-government is a demanding enterprise and perhaps we shouldn't automatically assume we are meeting its demands.

It may be we don't want to find out there is a question as to whether we are doing what our system requires of us. It may be that we don't want to risk having to admit we are *acting as if* we have given up on our system.

When are we *acting as if* we have given up? When a court gives four years in prison for robbery and attempted murder, are we *acting as if* we have given up on the hope of having a court system worthy of respect? When we assume we don't need to discuss domestic policy issues that we must understand, are we *acting as if* we have given up on self-government? If we don't try to see where we are going in foreign policy, whether we are "meddling" or "protecting our interests," are we *acting as if* we don't know and don't want to know what we are doing?

It would seem of paramount urgency to use communications media to discuss and attempt to identify those instances where we are *acting as if* we have given up. Besides discussing the ideas they express, influential experts should give us discussion to help us see those areas of responsibility where we no longer seem to be functioning as self-governing people. The danger is not that we will deliberately and visibly throw up our hands and declare we are quitting but that The Rules, the lack of dialogue, will allow us to move in the dark, to *act as if* we have given up without seeing it and admitting it.

If we don't ask questions, the decline of our institutions may go unmonitored until that decline is virtually impossible to reverse. It has happened elsewhere. It can happen here. What will matter in the end will not be our intentions. What will matter will be our actions.

When we see schools and libraries closed for lack of operating funds, or when we see college freshmen who can't read the directions for the use of a product, for whatever reason, it is a sign we have given up. When we assume the increasing demands on self-governing people can be met by semiliterates, our system isn't even working to sustain itself, let alone meet its responsibilities. If we don't assume this in our intentions, we assume it in our actions.

The frequent defeat of school budgets in many towns and cities seems to represent a blind lashing out against authority, to show conflict between school officials and the public. Lack of discussion and cooperation between parents and officials seems to result in costly hostilities. The quality of government services in general, and of education in particular, may indicate the interest or apathy of the public, the extent to which we have given up.

The final question is whether we will permit the politicians, scholars and experts to claim that public discussion is unworkable, impossible, too time-consuming or any number of other excuses. Most of the influential people seem willing to leave us largely excluded from the process of government and virtually stranded between their unexplained opposing views, with no clue as to which way to turn. We may not like the way things are going in our domestic and foreign policy but if we accept our continued exclusion from the process of government, we may have to admit that we deserve whatever we get.

If we don't insist on getting involved, we may have to admit that we deserve domestic and foreign policy that disappoints us, that we deserve bad regulation by government agencies, continued scandals in government agencies, bad legislation, bad education, higher taxes, all the things we think we have a right not to expect, all the things we think we don't deserve. However, the things we don't want to see happening are going to keep happening until we decide to get involved and get our leaders and thinkers to get involved with each other and with us.

The easy, comfortable thing for influential people to do is to continue to exclude us from our role and responsibility in government, to bump along as we have been, according to The Rules. The question is, how much longer will we permit them, and ourselves, to do the easy, comfortable thing?